When the Box is the Limit

WHEN THE BOX IS THE LIMIT

Drive your creativity
with constraints

WALTER VANDERVELDE

BIS Publishers

When the Box is the Limit
ISBN 978 90 6369 512 5

Copyright © 2018 Walter Vandervelde & BIS Publishers

www.whentheboxisthelimit.com

Copy Editors: Estelle Toscanucci, Bernandak and Tania Cohen
Research: Marc Heleven
Design: Walter Vandervelde

BIS Publishers
Building Het Sieraad
Postjesweg 1
1057 DT Amsterdam
The Netherlands
T +31 (0)20 515 02 30
bis@bispublishers.com
www.bispublishers.com

BIS PUBLISHERS

If you can't find
the solution
within the box,
you probably
haven't checked
all the corners.

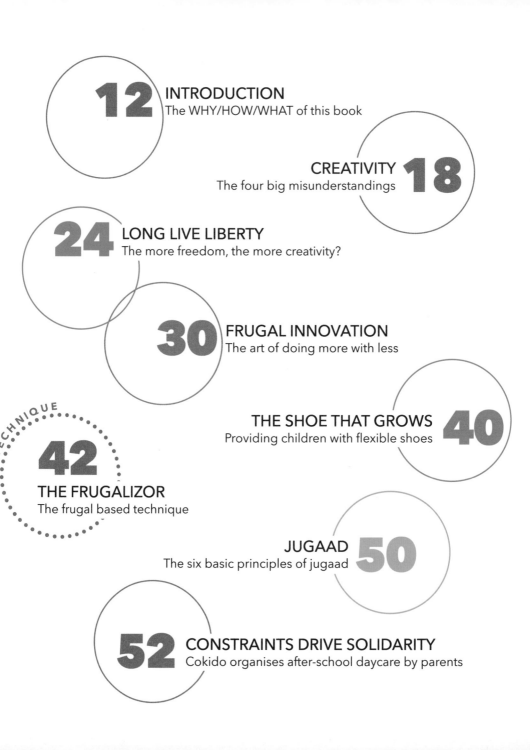

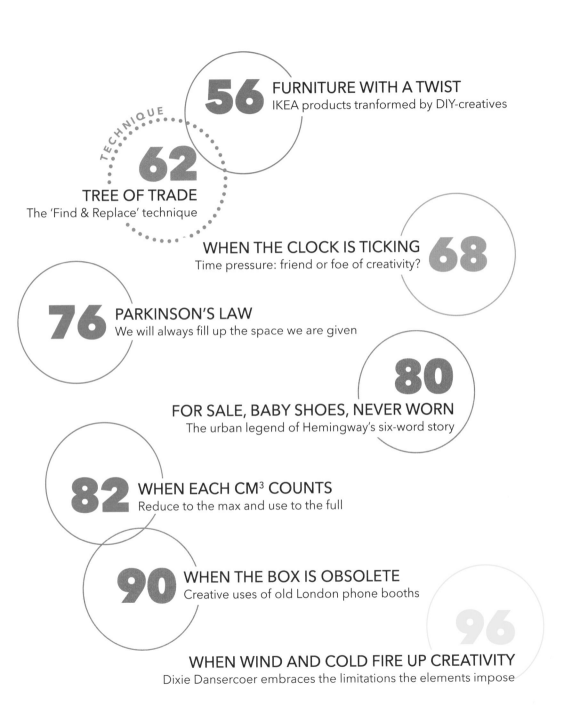

Introduction
The WHY/HOW/WHAT of this book

It has got to be one of the most well-known and most discussed business theories of the past few years: Simon Sinek's 'Golden Circle'. Explained in a nutshell, Sinek asserts that truly innovative and successful companies start their business operations by asking themselves the 'why'-question. Why do we do what we do? And why do we want to do that? What is our mission and what do we invariably believe in? A 'why' has to be inspiring, somewhat naïve even and with a clear message to make the world a better place. Only in the second and third phase the 'how' and 'what' questions can be asked. How are we going to live up to our 'why'? And what do we have to do, create, and offer to that end?

Despite the fact the Sinek's theory gets some heat of late, I still think it's a strong premise. And considering this book is primarily aimed at the business market, I'd like to use his methodology to put it in the right context.

WHY THIS BOOK?

Because creativity is vital. Because we think that creativity can only flourish without constraints. Because the previous sentence is a wrong assumption. Because a lot of people don't know how stimulating limitations can be. Because my knowledge and experience allow me to hand you the necessary tools for this. Because together we can make the world a better place… The wall of my home office is full of this sort of short 'because' sentences. On post-its of course, as the result of a real creativity session befits.

'When the box is the limit' is for all of us a daily reality, indeed. It is part and parcel of everything we do. From the place we were born to the talents we have been endowed with. From the time and the means we have at our disposal to the access to knowledge we think we need. There are boundaries to everything and to every action we take, every creative solution we think up will be subjected to a number of restrictive criteria. Just like I have to limit myself to 26 letters in this book, measurements of 200 x 170 mm, and 192 pages. And yet, I don't feel those as constraining, on the contrary. With 26 letters, I can convey in written form what I desire because I have been taught this as a child. The measurements of the book inspire me to find a balance between text and images because as a former designer I have practiced this a lot and have grown in mastering it. And finally, the 192 pages allow me to structure the book perfectly according to my wishes because I can

I have to limit myself to 26 letters in this book, measurements of 200 x 170 mm, and 192 pages. And yet, I don't feel those as constraining, on the contrary.

strategically plan it and, at the same time, be free to change the contents around, letting it come together as a jigsaw puzzle.

Short and sweet: I'm writing this book to convince you as a reader that restrictions can be very stimulating and, at the same time, hand you the tools to put it into practice.

HOW AM I GOING TO DO THAT?

I am not a reader. And I am not exactly proud of that. It is maybe a combination of being distracted easily and the fact that after two sentences I start to think how I could put the 'gained knowledge' into practice creatively. Yes, I do have books – because I truly love the tactile and visual aspect of them – and I also try my best to start reading them, but most of the time I fail to finish even the first thirty pages. Blame me.

Why do I tell you this? Because I really wanted to write a book, I would like to read myself. From cover to cover that is. Call it a kind of functional narcissism, but I have taken myself – the worst of readers – as a touchstone. So, what would intrigue me to finish reading a book? To start with: no academic-like, interminable texts. But a lot of pictures, sufficient white and imagery in the page lay-out, and easy-to-read typography. Short, standalone articles (because I can't read more than 5 minutes in one go), but still linked to each other thematically.

By a 'business' book, I also have to get inspired. It has to tickle my imagination, and I want to run with it too. So give me some tools, please, things I can really put into practice. And I want to have the possibility to discuss it with others, to share experiences. So, interactivity. Maybe I even want to add something to make the next edition still better? Yes, that's the sort of book that interests me. And that is what I want to write.

> So give me some tools, please, things I can really put into practice. And I want to have the possibility to discuss it with others, to share experiences.

WHAT DO I WANT TO DISH OUT TO YOU?

Maybe you have already leafed through the book, and I hope you liked your first impression of it. Or maybe you already read some bits and pieces here and there before you started on this preamble? Good, because that is point entirely. The book contains short bits of text that are completely self-contained, so you can read what you want, how much you want, and when you want. Just follow your instincts and let everything be determined by the moment.

And of course I have structured it, but maybe I did that more for myself. You know, limitations stimulate creativity. So, I don't even want to talk about the structure. However, I do want to talk about the contents. Evidently. As I have asserted above, I have three goals: *inspire, facilitate*, and **activate**.

I want to *inspire* by offering you a multitude of cases. Examples from a plethora of sectors, industries, and cultures from all over the world and from all eras. Some cases speak for themselves, with others I'll give some extra input on how you can use the featured case in your own situation. So, don't just be surprised by how and convinced of the fact that constraints stimulate creativity, but even more so, let it encourage you to get the most out of it for your own (business) world.

Even though the former already contains a piece of 'help you on your way', I want to really *facilitate* by handing you some creative techniques. You will find no less than five of them in this book. And each and every one of them is based on an analysis of 'best practices' (read: the cases) on the one hand, and my personal, professional experience with creativity techniques on the other. Especially for this book, I have put together a feedback team who have tested the techniques extensively. In this book itself, you will find the basic explanation of the technique, but if you really want to use it – solo or with your team – then you surf to the URL www.whentheboxisthelimit.com/techniques and there you will see related materials, like printable sheets, cards, and a more comprehensive manual, etc.

And this brings me seamlessly to the last goal I want to achieve: *activate*. This book is only the beginning. Not in the sense that I as a writer aim to write and market a whole series of sequels. No, my solo work stops here. I strongly believe in the power of collaboration which leads to open innovation, and we live in an amazing time that allows for that. I have created www.whentheboxisthelimit.com with the intention to make it a real community. Of and for people who are passionate about creativity and innovation, and are driven by curiosity and the need to improve things. I want to hear your own cases and best practices on the theme of creativity and restrictions, discover your points of improvement for the techniques – or maybe even totally new techniques -, listen to your questions, answers, insights, visions, and opinions. And I don't want to do that as an authority, but as a 'primus inter paris', a moderator who structures the box a little bit. An open box, for sure, that welcomes everybody.

I wish you lots of inspiration and insights, but most of all fun!

With love,

If you want to kill creativity, give someone total freedom, a blank page and a pen.

Creativity:
the four big **misunderstandings**

It still happens, even if I am thoroughly prepared for it by long years of experience. *'So, you are an artist?'* In an attempt to capture what one does professionally, people are often labeled easily but inaccurately. The label doesn't really fit the group of jobs but is tolerated because: *'he is able to make a living with it.'* I don't blame people. I tend to think that, to some extent, it may be even my own fault. But it is so darn difficult to explain in a few words to the man in the street that creativity – a profession I really do engage in – doesn't belong exclusively to the artistic world. Additionally, there are a lot of other things that can go awry when talking about creativity.

Granted, in the last few years the word has found its way into the corporate world more thoroughly than perhaps 15 years ago. And yet… a toe-curling feeling sneaks up on me every time I see photos on social media of so-called creative sessions where people are painting or clay modeling, where halls are decorated with garlands and balloons, and where crazy hats and confetti are flying. Don't get me wrong: there is nothing wrong with letting your hair down every once in a while, and with my students and trainees, I emphasize that a large dose of positivity and fun is the most important driver of intrinsic creativity. But creativity is so much more than that. That's why I want to put an end to four big misunderstandings about it once and for all.

"Creativity is tackling challenges, improving what exists today, and developing concepts determining our future."

'Creativity? Oh, what art do you practice?' As indicated above, this is probably the most entrenched thinking track when it comes to the word "creativity." And that is not surprising. One of the reasons for this misunderstanding is undoubtedly that the educational system in most countries is largely geared towards obtaining and reproducing knowledge. This is not surprising, because knowledge is measurable and quantifiable, and therefore easy to evaluate. Creativity is none of that – or at least much less so – and, consequently, plays a negligible role in most of the forms of education we know. You can find it in subjects like arts and crafts or musical education, and sometimes in literature, theatre or dance. These are all artistic expressions of creativity. There's nothing wrong with that, but creativity goes a lot further than just the artistic domain.

When we talk about creativity in a business or functional environment, then we primarily refer to tackling challenges, improving what exists today, and developing concepts determining our future. That is the kind of creativity that finds its outcome in new products and services, the improvement of processes and organizational forms, the way we live together, raise our kids, deal with conflicts or sometimes just how to create a new meal. In short, it is the motor of change and innovation, and the capacity to disrupt the status quo.

'Eureka, I have found it!' The myth of Archimedes, who – according to lore – ran naked through the streets of Syracuse after he discovered the volume displacement effect in his bathtub, is deeply rooted in our perception of problem-solving creativity. That one unique moment, the almost divine inspiration, unpredictable and uncontrollable; that is unfortunately how most people perceive the process of idea generation and consequently creativity in general.

We all know that aha-moment, but the sudden inspiration, that idea or solution

"Creativity doesn't end with an idea, however ingenious it may be. An idea is only a starting point. The end point is a concept - in the broadest sense of the word - that brings originality and value. And that is the best definition of creativity I can think of."

that seems to appear out of nowhere, is, in fact, the result of a preceding process. Usually a subconscious iterative process where an idea alternately occupies our mind and gets released. Through some stimulus – that we indeed often experience as unpredictable – the pieces fall together and we experience this as the spark that births the idea. Compare it with a crime investigation. It takes time for the detectives to have the pieces of the puzzle match, solve the case, and apprehend the perpetrator. You can hardly imagine that they wait passively hoping to get an unexpected inspiration that will solve the case miraculously. Yes, that hunch could appear at any given moment, but it would be worthless if the detectives didn't prepare thoroughly and have, so to speak, all the pieces of the puzzle on the table.

With creativity, it's no different. The creative process is one of falling down and getting back up, of daring to experiment, and getting out of your comfort zone. And, often, it is also a matter of hanging in there when the going gets tough and finishing what you started. Creativity doesn't end with an idea, however ingenious it may be. An idea is only a starting point. The end point is a concept - in the broadest sense of the word - that brings originality and value. And that is the best definition of creativity I can think of.

'Forget it! I'm not creative...' When, at the age of 48, I decided to do something about my physical health, cycling seemed like a good idea. Actually, it would never have occurred to me if a couple of friends – who made that wise decision a year earlier – hadn't motivated me to come along one Sunday morning in springtime. Let's be honest: it was drama, that first time. By nature, I am not the sporty type, and because of that, I have hardly ever engaged in sports. Panting and wheezing, I tried to keep up with my friends, but they had to wait for me every two kilometers. But as it goes with exercise, practice makes perfect, and every time I cycled, things improved. When I have a 'very good day' nowadays, I dare to leave the Peloton behind sometimes and wait for them proudly and satisfied at the next stop.

Why am I sharing this? Cycling or exercising in general don't really belong to my natural born talents. Before my 48th birthday, I had never really enjoyed it, and I looked at it as a necessary evil to keep somewhat fit. Moreover, it reminded me of my school years, when every damn morning began invariably with half an hour of cycling. But cycling in nature together with a couple of friends has changed that. The fun factor came into play, and that has motivated me enough to go on despite the difficult start. And from that, I conclude two things: you can improve your capability for cycling by practicing often, and the best motivation to go on is to enjoy it.

Replace the word 'cycling' with 'using creativity' or 'creative thinking', and you get the same story. Apart from the potential of the talent you are born with, you can lift your personal creativity to a higher level by practicing the creative process and by enjoying it. So, creativity is not the exclusive domain of people who are richly endowed with it at birth. What you have can be improved, like any other competency.

But creativity goes further than that. It is also a mindset, a way of thinking and acting. By adopting this mindset, creativity becomes a natural reflex that spurs positivity and problem-solving behavior.

CREATIVITY ≠ UNLIMITED FREEDOM

'Help, my creativity is blocked. Too many constraints!' For a lot of people, freedom and creativity go hand in hand. To create, you have to be free, because any restriction inhibits your creativity. This entrenched assumption also originates in the artistic world. People perceive an artist as a rebel who opposes all values, norms, and laws, and accepts no form of authority. That is a romantic vision, and while it is not totally without merit, it nonetheless has to be qualified. True, really innovative art needs a measure of revolt. Great artistic schools of thought have often grown out of frustration and discontent with established values and/or by experimenting with totally different forms of artistic expression.

In the world of applied creativity too, disruptive innovation demands a largely defiant attitude. But what we don't appreciate is that really groundbreaking ideas that lead to total renewal are rather rare. And in everyday life, creativity is usually about an incremental improvement of what already exists, and the circumstances we work in are anything but limitless. In other words, reality forces us to take limits and constraints of any nature into account. Accepting these limits is often freeing and inspiring, because who would want to start with a blank page every day?

This book is about this last misunderstanding. Total freedom is a fallacy, but that doesn't have to be a downer to our creativity. On the contrary, limitations can be liberating and have a stimulating effect. They give us structure and put us in the cage that we often need in order to come up with strong, original ideas.

"Accepting these limits is often freeing and inspiring, because who would want to start with a blank page every day?"

LONG LIVE
LIBERTY

The more **freedom,** the more **creativity**?

When we talk about the creative process, we think subconsciously of the divergent phase where ideas go in all different directions, freely and without limits. We assume that total freedom and unlimited means are the only ways to come up with cutting edge ideas that lead to successful innovation. These are suppositions that find their origins in how we think artistic creativity works. We imagine artists as rebels who kick established values in the shins and only come to useful creation when all borders and limitations have fallen by the wayside. Thinking out of the box is an expression that is inseparably connected to creativity, because, above all, we want to wriggle ourselves out of that straightjacket of rules and agreements to become original and, if need be, reinvent the world. The sky is the limit, right?

The thought that constraints hamper our creativity is deeply rooted. It is the explanation we like to give when we don't get our desired results in solving a problem. *'Yes, but I needed more means, or more time, or more insight, or more space….'* This explanation can quickly become an excuse, an escape route to avoid certain challenges and resign ourselves. That's not only a pity, but unjustified. Indeed, several studies prove the opposite: creativity, in the form of original and valuable ideas, often springs up from limitations.

A great number of artists of much renown know all too well how paralyzing the idea of 'the blank page' is. Total freedom doesn't inspire. That's why many artists like to limit themselves. Think of the world of poetry with its different verse forms like the haiku, limerick, and sonnet.

The strict, established rules of the format become a framework within which the poet has to deliver his message. As such, the rules with which their work has to comply become a creative challenge. And that challenge is often needed to bring out the artist's full creative potential.

For instance, consider one of the most well-known sculptures in the world: David by Michelangelo. Connoisseurs claim that the artist would have never made such a powerful and admirable work had he worked with soft clay, which is much easier to handle. It is exactly because of the simultaneous unmanageability and fragility of the marble as a working material that the artist was able to bring out the best in himself.

The famous American architect and furniture designer Charles Eames assumed that creativity is in large part the result of limitations. He even claimed that a designer's success or failure is dependent on the measure of 'willingness and enthusiasm' with which they work under given limitations.

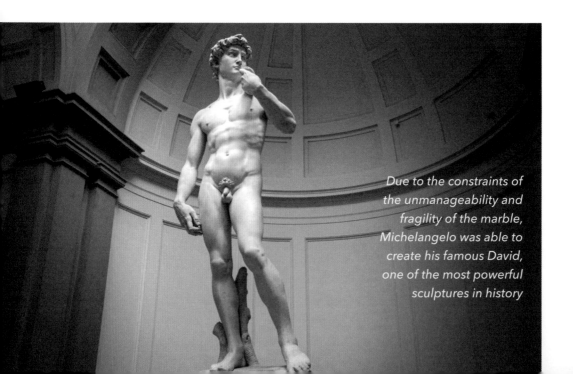

Due to the constraints of the unmanageability and fragility of the marble, Michelangelo was able to create his famous David, one of the most powerful sculptures in history

In the world of music, Russian composer Igor Stravinsky writes "... *my freedom will be so much the greater and more meaningful the more narrowly I limit my field of action, and the more I surround myself with obstacles. The more constraints one imposes, the more one frees oneself of the claims that shackle the spirit.*" Stravinsky loved to play around with musical composition by using self-imposed constraints. In some works, he elected to use certain pitches only, while in others he limited the technical demands on the performer, and so on. Sometimes, those problems were even technological in nature: Stravinsky's Serenade in A for Piano (1925) was composed with the particular limitations of a 78-rpm record in mind. To be able to fit it on a single side of the record, each of the four movements is around three minutes long.

As a graphic designer and, later on, creative director, I have often seen how strongly limitations can fuel one's creativity.

No time for an expensive photo shoot? Then you just work with a few strong words and some beautiful typography or a simple graphic. No budget for advertising? Then you design a campaign so creative it goes viral.

These limitations most often stemmed from the client. Sometimes budgets were very small, but the client nonetheless wanted maximum impact of their communication campaign. Recognizable? In such a case, as a designer, you look for alternatives and turn your creative brain to maximum speed. No time for an expensive photo shoot? Then you just work with a few strong words and some beautiful typography or a simple graphic. No budget for advertising? Then you design a campaign so creative it goes viral. The same holds true when time becomes a constraint. Deadline tomorrow? Then you throw all dead weight overboard and keep focused as much as possible. During this time in my life, I came to fully understand and embrace the expression 'less is more.' My definition of a good designer also evolved: someone who can achieve maximum impact employing minimum means.

Limitations liberate, while freedom limits. A lot of artists and creative professionals will endorse this paradox even though most people will intuitively think the opposite. But how is it that total freedom and lack of any structure or limitation result in paralysis? In many cases, this has to do with the stress of choice. In psychology, the phenomenon is known as 'The tyranny of choice.' Studies show that the more choices you have, the more difficult it becomes to decide. This results from the anticipation of regret that grows with every option. If we make a choice, how can we be sure this is the right one or the best one? In other words, choosing becomes losing and we want to prevent that at all costs, so we choose not to make a choice and circumvent the very phenomenon of the blank page. This way, they can bring us 'in the flow', because often the first step in a creative process is the hardest.

> Limitations liberate, while freedom limits. A lot of artists and creative professionals will endorse this paradox even though most people will intuitively think the opposite.

But before we rush in, one more thing: not all limitations are liberating. An excess of limitations, for instance, can demotivate and paralyze. A repetition of the same limitation(s) won't stimulate our creativity endlessly either. You can also give people too little time, budget or means and exclude any alternative solution right from the beginning. Too much is too much; often, the trick is finding the right balance. And that, of course, is also dependent on the level at which someone can employ their creativity. People with more experience can handle some initial limitations, while you would probably limit such demands on people that are less creatively experienced.

That the idea of 'liberating limitations' has reached the corporate world is proven by CEO of Yahoo Marissa Mayer's quote: *'Creativity loves constraints.'* But she also adds carefully: '... *but they must be balanced with a healthy disregard for the impossible.'* I couldn't agree more because asserting that creative ideas only spring from constraints would be completely wrong. Again, balance is crucial here.

"The more constraints one imposes,
the more one frees oneself of the
claims that shackle the spirit."

Igor Stravinksy
Russian composer, pianist and conductor

FRUGAL
INNOVATION

The art of doing
more with less

Every year, billions of dollars are spent on R&D, by the big kahunas in Silicon Valley that are perpetually searching for 'the next big thing,' as well as by the business world at large. They hire the best minds, put heavy pressure on competitors, and, if necessary, exhaust natural resources to stay on top in this endless rat race. But what are they really trying to market? Products with more possibilities than ever before and that are sold at ever higher prices, but that truthfully, very few people need. Of course, the shareholders want to see money. Innovation is a function of profit, because that's how the business model works.

An increasing number of companies are realizing that this profit model is untenable in the long run. There are a few reasons for this change in philosophy. Firstly, the consumer can't spend forever. Maybe there will always be an elite who has the purchasing power and is crazy enough to do just that, but it's not the critical mass that is necessary to generate profits year after year. Secondly, the natural resources - most importantly, water and oil - used for production purposes are finite. And finally, as a manufacturer, you cannot create needs endlessly. Eventually, you will arrive at a saturation point and the pendulum will invariably swing the other way.

Picture on the left
TAHMO is a network of affordable weather stations in Sub Saharan Africa to inform local farmers on upcomung weather conditions.

Creativity is about making life better

And that movement starts today. Motivated by a growing ecological and social consciousness, start-ups are looking for ways of doing more with less. They prefer to forgo extremely expensive research teams and look for meaning. And they are finding it in areas dismissed for years; mainly in the 'poor' countries in the Global South or so-called 'emerging markets'. Scarcity of means, money, and know-how – or sometimes even extreme circumstances like hunger or war – forces people to make the most of what's at hand. This is what is called 'frugal innovation'. It is the kind of innovation that is in stark contrast to what we in the West have become accustomed to. It's having no highly educated engineers, no exceedingly expensive test labs, and certainly no predator investors trying to make money fast. No, these are ordinary people, often without any formal education, with the street as their R&D lab. They are people who have but one use for creativity and innovation: making life better.

In his book *'Frugal Innovation: How to do more with less'*, Navi Radjou gives many examples. What would you make of a fridge made out of clay, that uses no electricity, and still manages to keep fruits and vegetables fresh for days? Mansukh

A fridge that uses no elecricity but still keeps food fresh for several days.

Prajapati, the Indian designer, is not driven by profit, and has but one goal: *'I wanted to make a product that poor people could afford and that is not harmful to the environment.'* This device is offered for less than €40. And how about the ingenuity of the next innovation: a billboard that takes water from the air and turns it into drinking water. In Lima, Peru, where despite high humidity the climate is characterized by long periods of draught, this innovation is a godsend. The billboard can generate approximately 90 liters of drinking water per day.

Often, innovations addressing a very local need find their way to areas with similar needs and quickly reach a lot of people using few means. In Kenya, for instance, today about half the population uses M-PESA, a mobile payment system. Actually, in all of Africa, where 80% of the population doesn't have a bank account but does own a mobile phone, there is a great need for this. But even more important are the potential secondary benefits of these kinds of products and services. From M-PESA emerged another innovation, M-KOPA, an all-in-one package deal for comprehensive household energy supply. The latter is an all-in-one package deal for an all-round household energy supply. It contains a set of solar panels,

A billboard that transforms air into 90 liters of drinking water a day.

three LED lamps, a radio, and a mobile phone on solar power. The package costs €200, which is quite a lot of money for the local population but is doable for most people by paying with regular micropayments made possible by the M-PESA service rather than paying the entire sum at once. Using this method, today almost 500.000 families from Kenya, Tanzania, and Uganda enjoy their own energy supply. This is undoubtedly a good

M-KOPA is an all-in-one package deal for a comprehensive household energy supply.

example of how frugal innovation utilizes what is available (mobile phones) and uses that resource to provide a solution for what is scarce (access to an affordable energy supply).

Another great example of frugal innovation is The Trans-African HydroMeteorological Observatory (TAHMO). Although weather data improve the lives of many people, there are still parts of the globe where weather monitoring doesn't exist. That is exactly the case across much of the African continent. TAHMO is an initiative aimed at rolling out a network of 20,000 affordable weather stations in Sub Saharan Africa. This monitoring network will replace a rapidly deteriorating system, and it's

The weather information from the TAHMO stations is crucial for African farmers

expected to be a vital tool for tracking climate change in the continent. The weather information retrieved from the stations will be converted to weather information services for farmers.

Learning and applying

Fortunately, in richer countries, the idea that doing more with less could be the model for the future is slowly but surely gaining traction. A growing number of innovative Western start-ups with mindsets not only focused on profit are becoming inspired by the creativity that frugal innovation brings. For instance, Be-Bound developed a device that grants internet access without WIFI, 3G or 4G just by making use of basic SMS/texting technology. This basic technology is more reliable than the other three anyway

Be-Bound offers internet access without WIFI, 3G, or 4G

and is more accessible around the world. Knowing that almost half of the world's population today has no Internet access, this technology offers an easy solution with very low costs.

There is also growing number of customers for frugally innovative solutions in the West. One example is the success of the cheap Logan-range of Renault-Dacia. In Europe, there is a sizeable demand for frugal solutions,

The Dacia Logan (by Renault) starts at ± €5.000

and not only in the emerging markets of Eastern-Europe but also from consumers in the Western, Northern, and Southern parts of Europe. Whereas enlarging the existing means is an important driver of demand, smart solutions can appeal to consumers who are looking for organic and 'ethical' products. Instead of assuming that frugal innovation only applies to certain groups of consumers, it may be smarter to see it in the light of what economists call 'high elasticity of demand'. This is most certainly the case when it is about products where, by crossing a particular threshold, a price cut (based on a more focused functionality) will lead to a strong rise in demand.

It is crucial that frugal innovation offers solutions that are not only cheaper but also better. This is achieved by focusing on users' needs and by drastically prioritizing functions that are of singular importance to customers. To that end, with frugal innovation one must sometimes reinvent a product or solution that already exists in another form. Concretely, frugality can be achieved in several ways. These ways include: de-featuring (taking away unnecessary functions of an existing product), enhancing the robustness and durability of a product to extend its life, improving the efficiency of manufacturing processes and supply chains or using resources more efficiently (for instance by improving the product's design), using waste products in a circular economy model, or rethinking how often-hidden assets (including people) can be put to good use. And the very process of innovation itself can also be made more frugal, for instance by crowdsourcing ideas instead of utilizing traditional R&D processes.

"Instead of assuming that frugal innovation only applies to certain groups of consumers, it may be smarter to see it in the light of what economists call 'high elasticity of demand'."

LEARNINGS & IDEAS

This is your free space to reflect on what the previous story might have taught you and how you can use this knowledge in your own (work) environment. Let the questions here below stimulate you, take a pen and start writing!

- Do you have the social and ecological courage to go frugal?
- Is there a potential market for your products and/or services of people with less means that you can service?
- Are you in a price battle with your competitors and could frugal innovation be a possible solution?

WHEN LIFE GIVES YOU
LEMONS,
MAKE
MARGARITAS

THE SHOE THAT GROWS

While writing this text, I took a look at the website of the organization 'The Shoe That Grows." '145,586 pairs of shoes distributed, 926 distribution partners in 97 countries,' it says. These numbers don't surprise me one bit, because the organization has conjured up and marketed a splendid product: shoes that grow with the child.

Worldwide there are about 300 million children who don't have shoes. This is not only a problem of comfort, but even more so, one of health. Walking barefoot exposes children to the danger of becoming injured or contracting parasites that infect the body through the feet, making them ill and sometimes resulting in death. The additional challenge, of course, is that children grow fast and need new shoes almost every year. That demand is hardly ever met.

'The design process was very interesting,' says inventor **Kenton Lee**, 'even more so because I am not a designer at all. Even worse, I didn't know anything about shoes. I was just a guy with an idea.' And that idea was so simple that you ask yourself why nobody ever came up with it before. The shoe is more of an open sandal and, as a user, you can adjust it in three spots in a jiffy, so it always fits around your foot. One pair of sandals will last children five years. That means that the materials should be robust. 'We have never skimped on quality,' Lee says. 'The sole is made of compressed rubber (comparable to car tires), and the rest of the shoe is made of high quality leather. Therefore, we go for high quality and sustainable materials only.'

Inventor Kenton Lee is not a designer, but just a guy with a great idea who had the courage to persist in solving a problem that is changing the lives of millions of children.

THE
FRUGA
LIZOR

The frugal based technique:
The Frugalizor

TECHNIQUE IN BRIEF ON PAGE 180

The Frugalizor is a technique inspired by the principles of frugal innovation. By analyzing many of the inspiring stories I came across, there were a number of underlying mechanisms that always came back. In this technique, I have carefully selected 12 of those mechanisms which might help you to enhance innovating your personal subject.

Note that - in order to give the concept a unique touch - most of the names I have given to the specific mechanisms are non-existing words. For instance 'DIYING' comes from 'DIY' or 'Do-It-Yourself'. 'USERAIZING' is a combination 'user' and 'raising', meaning that you have to raise the number of users. 'BELTIZING', because the purpose is to investigate how you can make your subject easily adaptable to the user, like a belt. Etc.

Also be aware that when I use the word 'subject' in the description of the mechanisms, I mean it in its broadest sense. In other words, a 'subject' can be a concrete product, a service, a process, a structure as well as an idea, a design, a vision or any other form of innovation issue you are working on.

You can apply this technique all by yourself, but like many other techniques, it's way more fun and much more rewarding to do this in a group. You can download the PDF-file of the graphs free of charge at www.whentheboxisthelimit.com/frugalizor or scan the QR-code on the left.

How it works:

STEP 1

- Print the tools you downloaded previously on www. whentheboxisthelimit.com/ techniques/frugalizor

- There are two tools:

  - The poster (The Frugalizor poster.pdf), which you should print on an A2 size or bigger and hang it on the wall

  - The 12 mechanisms (The Frugalizor tent cards.pdf), which you should print on thick paper (at least 200 gr) on A4 size, fold them in two and put them on the table as a tent card

- Let the participants sit around the table. The bigger the group, the better (ideally at least 8 people, but less is also possible). I suggest you work in teams of at least two people.

- Give each team a sufficient number of post-its.

STEP 2

- Each team now chooses one or more tent cards to put in front of them on the table.

- During five to ten minutes (depending on the number of cards each team has chosen), each team comes up with as many ideas as possible related to the mechanism on the tent card(s).

- All ideas are written on post-its and pasted on the table for the time being

- When the time is up, the teams stop generating ideas.

STEP 3

- Repeat STEP 2, but with new tent cards per team.

- Of course, when some mechanisms / tent cards have not yet been dealt with, they are given priority. In case they have all been treated, they are simply interchanged between the teams.

STEP 4

- *You decide how many rounds of idea generating you need and when you're done, all the ideas on the post-its should be attached to the Frugalizor poster.*

- *The best ideas will be worked out.*

On the next pages, you will discover the 12 mechanisms of The Frugalizor (which are also mentioned on the tent cards).

DEFEATURING

1. Make a list of all the features and elements of your subject.

2. Start by eliminating the less substantial ones and ask yourself with each elimination whether the subject still 'works'.

3. Continue doing this until you get to a subject stripped to its absolute minimal viability.

DIYING

1. Make a list of the steps that make up your subject, the materials, and/or actions involved.

2. Ask yourself which of the steps, materials or actions the users themselves can take care of.

MULTIPURPOSING

1. Make a random list of as many other industries and markets different from your target industry or market.

2. Ask yourself if your subject could be used in one of these other industries/markets and for which purpose.

3. Or the other way around: start with thinking for which other purposes your subject could also be suitable and then link them to their specific industries or markets.

USERAIZING

1. Define the initial target audience of your subject and describe specifically why this audience uses your subject.

2. Now make your target audience more inclusive incrementally and with each increment, see how you have to adapt your subject.

3. Note: When adapting your subject, try to avoid adding features or elements to it.

BELTIZING

1. Think up ideas how you can make your subject 'one size fits all' for all your users.

and/or

2. Think up ideas how you can make your subject easily adaptable for each user's specific requirements (adjustable like a belt).

LOCALIZING

1. List all the materials your subject is composed of.

2. List all the services that come with your subject.

3. List all the steps of the production and logistics process of your subject.

4. Check all items on the three lists one by one and ask yourself which of these could be taken care of locally with resources that are at hand.

ECOLOGIZING

1. Ask yourself how you can proof your subject to become more ecologically safe throughout its entire life cycle.

2. To make it easier, you could use a waste hierarchy pyramid *(check on the downloadable tent card).*

ECONOMIZING

1. Make a list of all consumption and running costs of your subject on the user's side.

2. Ask yourself which of these costs can be lowered or eliminated, and how to do this.

ROBUSTING

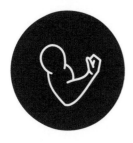

1. Ask yourself how you can make your subject more robust, durable, and reliable.

CROWDSOURCERING

1. Ask yourself how you can use and maximize the input of the (local) crowd to design, develop, and/or enhance your subject.

UNLINKING

1. Make separate lists for all the production, action, process, administration, and/or distribution steps/links of your subject.

2. For each step/link on each list, ask yourself whether it can be skipped and eliminated.

DECOSTING

1. Ask yourself randomly in which (other) ways you can lower production, process or service cost of your subject to decrease the price for the end-user.

2. Note: chances are that you come up with ideas that will also be driven by one of the other mechanisms, but we won't let any chance for a great new idea pass, will we?

Some sources claim that **Frugal** finds its origin in **Jugaad**. Other sources call Jugaad part of Frugal. Either way, they are closely related concepts. Together with other concepts – like Grassroots innovation, Ghandian innovation or Reverse innovation – they are used interchangeably and by and large address the same subjects.

Jugaad finds its origins in **India** and followers claim that it is deeply engrained in the DNA of its population. By applying the Jugaad philosophy, new companies grew out of creative ideas and inventive slum dwellers became small entrepreneurs. Based on a number of case studies, six basic principles of these success stories emerged. You will find them on the opposite page.

The six basic principles of
JUGAAD

1. Seek the opportunity in adversity

Jugaad entrepreneurs look at harsh constraints as a challenge to innovate. For example, a man was tired of riding his bike on bumpy roads. To make the situation work for him, he decided to connect his bike to a device that transformed the shocks into acceleration energy. By doing this, he took advantage of the bumpy roads rather than having to suffer them.

2. Do more with less

Optimize the use of scarce commodities and deliver more value to more customers. Jugaad innovators work with what's at hand. This sober 'less is more' principle teaches us to optimize the use of scarce financial and natural resources while also delivering high value.

3. Think and act flexibly

The flexible mindset of Jugaad innovators continuously challenges the status quo and keeps all options open, thereby transforming existing products, services, and business models. They avoid the beaten tracks and are masters in thinking and acting in alternatives.

4. Keep it simple

With Jugaad, it isn't about looking for refinement or perfection by (technologically) over-developing products, but thinking of "good enough" solutions that get the job done. People are often in greater need of user-friendliness than of extra features.

5. Include the margin

Jugaad innovators are not interested in mainstream consumers. Rather, they consciously look for consumers in the margins who typically aren't catered to in product development. Through innovation, they want to better integrate excluded groups into mainstream society.

6. Follow your heart

In the Jugaad world, you won't come across focus groups or extended market research. You also won't find major strategies or traditional business models. Jugaad innovators are closely connected to their customers as well as their products and services, so they tend to go with their gut more often.

CONSTRAINTS

DRIVE

SOLIDARITY

Cokido organizes after-school daycare by parents

Admit it, in most European countries we are spoiled rotten by the state. And we don't always realize it. When we are sick, the doctor is there. When we suddenly lose our job, we may be able to get welfare. And if there is a school holiday or if we have to work overtime, we just dump our children in the after-school daycare, don't we?

But what if the latter is not possible? That's what happened to Eefje Cottenier, a young Belgian mother. She was too late applying for daycare and couldn't find childcare when she needed it. A handful of other parents found themselves in the same situation as her, and so the search for a creative solution began.

Cokido is proof that creativity and solidarity make strong partners when circumstances are unfavorable. The basic concept is simple: in exchange for minding other people's children one day a week, the other four workdays your children are taken care of by other participants. With some organization and a little bit of goodwill, the parents managed to make it work. In no time at all, this local project traveled to other cities

Eefje Cottenier: "'The autonomy we offer to local groups of parents is very important. This way, a spontaneous form of creativity arises that we can often learn from ourselves."

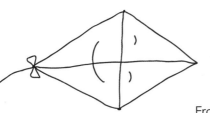

and today – not even a year after the concept spread – hundreds of families use Cokido successfully.

From the beginning, the social aspect of Cokido played an important role. Co-creation lies at the root of the idea, but it doesn't stop there. Often, children are the social glue between adults in a community. You notice that all the more at Cokido. Parents who are struggling to integrate into the language and culture have the opportunity for social integration in a very natural way by cooperating with other parents. A network of trust develops, because, in the end, it's all about the highest good: the children.

The strange thing about this concept is that the government – whose shortcomings led to the idea's development in the first place – is now trying to integrate the idea into the existing options for childcare. Local administrators and businesses also started to participate, and that became the foundation of the business model: the lowest possible cost for the parents by finding ways to utilize all means in the most creative way. For instance, partners were sought to supply sustainable furniture and toys in a rotating model.

Cokido deliberately stays true to its two basic principles: creativity and solidarity. The organization offers a basic open platform (also as a digital app) that is shaped by the parents according to their needs. The emergent creativity inspired them to improve the concept in its own right. In this way, a natural process of continuous improvement based on a foundation of trust and solidarity ensues.

More about Cokido at www.cokido.be (only in Dutch)

LEARNINGS & IDEAS

This is your free space to reflect on what the previous story might have taught you and how you can use this knowledge in your own (work) environment. Let the questions here below stimulate you, take a pen and start writing!

- Are you dependent on many third parties to do your daily business? And what if a crucial party would suddenly disappear? How do you fill that gap?
- Can you count on solidarity from people in the same situation? And how will you organise this?

FURNITURE
WITH A TWIST

Function should not be constrained by form

IKEA products transformed by DIY-creatives

What's the first thing that comes to mind when you think of the words 'box' and 'furniture'? You probably didn't have to think long: IKEA it is! The furniture giant owes its success to four factors: design, affordability, vicinity, and shop experience. As a result, it gained an unheard of degree of market penetration. A house without any IKEA products is hard to find. You don't have to like IKEA, but you do have to admit that they have shaken up the furniture and home décor market.

The IKEA case actually provides a great answer to the title of this book: *When the box is the limit... you have to deliver the goods unassembled.* Assembling a piece of IKEA furniture has gained something of an iconic status, and everyone has a personal anecdote to share. Just like that small collection of 'missing' nuts and bolts in the back of some drawer that hopelessly awaits the moment it will ever come in handy.

The fun of IKEA's assembly principle is that many creative DIYers have found the inspiration to make smart alternatives using IKEA products, whether thinking of new functions, pimping the designs, or transforming the products into veritable works of art. If you Google 'IKEA Hacks,' you will be surprised by the endless ideas that people seem to have.

What to think of a wine rack that – just by turning it 90 degrees – suddenly becomes a handy plant pot holder *(see picture 1)*?

Picture 1: A wine rack becomes an elegant plant pot holder by simply turning it 90°

Picture 2: A classic IKEA pine dresser becomes a fancy piece of furniture after some coloring and decoration

Or a boring pine dresser that looks a lot more charming after some coloring and decoration work *(see picture 2)*?

Things can get even more inventive, like a modulated coffee table made out of binders *(see picture 3)* or a children's wooden walking bicycle made primarily out of bar stool parts *(see picture 4)*.

A beautiful example of how you can transform a simple piece of furniture into a quasi-work of art that still proves extremely functional is the Mandala bookcase *(see picture 5)*. And it gets even crazier when decorative elements get a practical function, like the bathroom wall in an Amsterdam loft that is comprised exclusively of IKEA

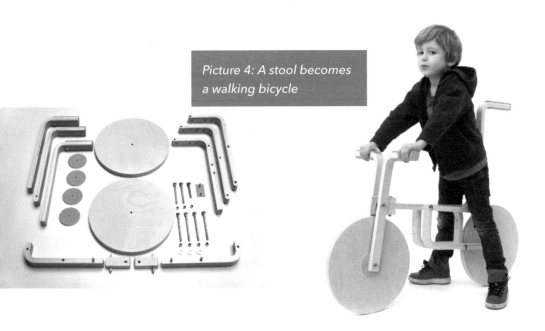

Picture 4: A stool becomes a walking bicycle

Rektangel vases *(see picture 6).* And there are hundreds of other clever and creative examples to be found.

In short, it is amazing what people can create using existing products. The possibilities are limitless, even if the contents of 'the box' are limited. Undoubtedly, the motivation to repurpose these products stems largely from the fact that the products still have to be assembled anyway. In other words, you don't have to disassemble products to

Picture 5: The Mandala bookcase shows a beautiful mariage of art and functionality

make something new from them. It's enough to assemble something in a different way, to combine the elements of different 'boxes' and/or spruce up materials by painting them, varnishing them, decorating them, etc.

It reminds me of an exercise that I use regularly in training environments to teach the power of 'seeing differently,' which, of course, is one of the basic skills of creative thinking. I divide the group into small subgroups of 3 or 4 people, give each subgroup an everyday object, and ask them to think of at least 10 new functions for that object that are different from the original function.

After all the groups present their new ideas, I ask them to select the most creative function. Then, I put the subgroups to work adjusting the object in such a way that it is even better suited for its new function. The results are often mind-blowing and on occasion, the groups are so fired up that they organize an extra session to develop their concept even more.

At the same time, this exercise is a way to work with limitations: how far can you go in thinking up and creating alternatives from the elements at hand? In the case of the IKEA hacks, the box becomes a muse, or at least the contents of it. It again proves how a limitation – here in the form of a finite amount of elements as a starting point – can lead to ideas and solutions that otherwise might never have been.

Picture 6: A bathroom wall made up exclusively of IKEA Rektangel vases

The 'Find & Replace' technique:
Tree of Trade

TECHNIQUE IN BRIEF ON PAGE 181

Limitations often are incredibly powerful in stimulating creativity, because they force us to think laterally, in alternatives. And, as it turns out, that is the very difference between a linear and a creative thinker: where the first group is satisfied with only one solution – even though it is the obvious way to go and consequently not really innovative – the second group will only be satisfied when there is more than one idea on the table. That means that numerous alternative ideas are evaluated, selected, combined, and enhanced to come to a totally new solution in the end.

Tree of Trade is a technique that is built on thinking in alternatives. We start with listing the essential elements that are inherent to the question, look at the needs they fulfill, and, afterwards, try to find alternative elements that cater to the same needs. In the last step, we will – if necessary – translate those elements realistically so that they result in genuinely useful solutions.

You can apply this technique all by yourself, but like many other techniques, it's way more fun and much more rewarding to do this in a group. You can download the PDF-file of the graph free of charge at www.whentheboxisthelimit.com/treeoftrade or scan the QR-code on the left.

How it works:

STEP 1

- Print the graph more than once in a big size, minimum A2, but bigger is better, certainly when you work in a group.

- Put the first graph on the table or hang it on the wall. See what works best for you.

- Provide post-its and markers for all participants.

STEP 2

- Discuss the central question or problem, and ensure that everyone understands it clearly. Write the problems down if necessary and keep them visible during the entire process.

- From this question or problem, try to distill a list of as many elements as possible that are associated with the respective issue or problem.

- Keep this list of elements at hand or stick it on the wall.

STEP 3

- Take one element from the list, write it on a post-it, and stick it in the circle 'MISSING ESSENTIAL' of the first graph.

STEP 4

- With the group, discuss which need this element fulfills with regard to the issue or problem.

- Write that need on a post-it and stick it in the circle 'RELATED NEED'.

- If the corresponding element fulfills more than one need, use multiple graphs and stick one need in the circle 'RELATED NEED' per graph (while in the meantime also filling the circle 'MISSING ESSENTIAL' on every graph you work on).

STEP 5

- Now together look for which other or alternative elements can fulfill this need with an eye to your question or problem. You can take this as far as you want. Definitely, don't stop at self-evident solutions.

- Select the four most original ideas and stick those in the respective circles 'ALTERNATIVE A, B, C, D'.

- Do the same for the other graphs if there are any.

- Sometimes these elements offer the right alternative solution immediately, but not always. In the latter case proceed to step 6.

STEP 6

- Focus on the issue or problem and see how you can translate the post-its stuck in the respective circles 'ALTERNATIVE A, B, C, D' to an actionable idea.

- Try to find at least three "translations" per alternative, write them down on the post-its and stick those in the circles 'TRANSLATION 1, 2, AND 3'.

STEP 7

- Go back to step 3 and repeat until you have covered the entire list of elements.

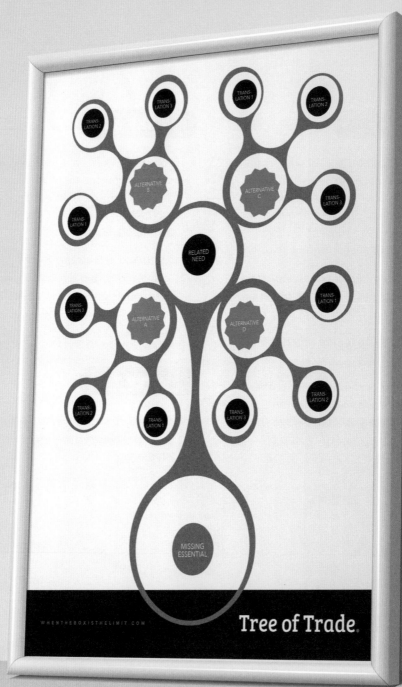

"Art consists in limitation. The most beautiful part of every picture is the frame."

G. K. Chesterton,
English writer, poet and philosopher

WHEN THE
CLOCK
IS TICKING

Time Pressure:
friend or foe of creativity?

Time is money, so time is precious. You can waste time or lose it, and lost time can never be recovered because you can't turn back the clock... These are all universal wisdoms and expressions we hardly ever contemplate anymore. But what is the relationship between time and creativity? Is time pressure – and, as a consequence, stress – one of the biggest idea killers or do you need a good dose of stress to come up with awesome ideas? As with many things: the truth lies somewhere in the middle. Based on Braden Becker's article *'The Surprising Relationship Between Stress and Creativity'*, I want to give you a look into three kinds of pressure that is related to time. It is important to look at each of those in detail to thoroughly understand the relationship between time and creativity.

1. The Switch

Suppose they ask you to solve three problems within an hour. How would you go about it? Or in other words: how are you going to split your time between the three? Here are three possibilities:

- **Option A:**
  You take exactly 20 minutes for each problem and during that time you concentrate on that problem exclusively.

- **Option B:**
  You take regular intervals – say 5 minutes – to go from one problem to the next. So you never think about the same problem for more than 5 minutes at a time.

- **Option C:**
  During that full hour, you switch from problem to problem as you see fit.

Most people choose option C. Of course – you think – because you know best when you get stuck on one problem and want to move on to the next? We find autonomy and flexibility are very important when it comes to creative problem solving. Wrong, as it turns out… A 2017 study about Organizational Behavior and Human Decision processes tells us that we are not always aware we got stuck on a particular problem. So we usually don't know when it is time to move on to the next problem. By switching regularly, you subconsciously force yourself to approach the problem from different angles. Therefore, option B is the right answer. By switching regularly, you subconsciously force yourself to approach the problem from another starting phase and hence a different angle. This way of working boosts creativity and prevents the 'rigid thinking' that can occur when you focus on the same problem too long. We have all encountered this situation at one point or another.

2. The Constructive Challenge

In the 2015 study *'Job Stressors, Organizational Innovation Climate, and Employees' Innovative Behavior'*, two Chinese researchers studied different forms of stress and their influence on our creativity. They came to the conclusion that not all forms of stress impaired the generation of valuable ideas. For instance, stressors that are interpreted as constructive and challenging for the final assignment that has to be completed have a positive effect on creativity. The reverse is true for stressors that are perceived as impeding or precluding execution of the assignment. It is a theory that actually had been suggested a few years before by Teresa Amabile, professor at Harvard Business School and one of the most renowned experts worldwide in the study of creative behavior. In her book *'The Progress Principle'* she places four forms of stress in a matrix that is defined by two axes: work or time pressure and importance/meaning. She defines the stress forms as follows:

- **The treadmill:**
  You work under high pressure, but the assignment is of little importance or meaning.

- **The automatic pilot:**
  You work under low pressure, and the assignment is of little importance or meaning.

- **The expedition:**
  You work under low pressure, but the assignment is of great importance or meaning.

- **The mission:**
  You work under high pressure, and the assignment is of great importance or meaning.

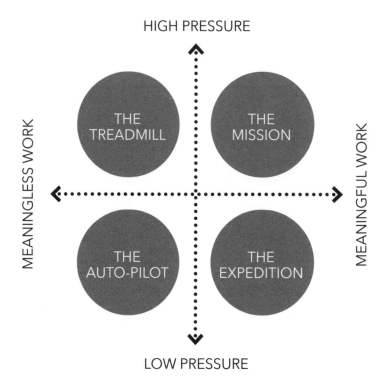

'The treadmill' as well as 'the automatic pilot' are very repetitive and therefore less attractive which means there is little creativity needed. 'The expedition' and 'the mission' on the contrary are important and meaningful, and this is exactly what sparks creativity, according to Amabile. When you reach a goal that you perceive as meaningful, you start to feel good, and your self-confidence soars. That motivates you to start on a new task.

The relationship between time pressure and creativity is dependent on how you perceive that pressure at any given moment. If that pressure is meaningful and important to reach the ultimate objective of the assignment, then it will ignite and stimulate your creativity. If the pressure is perceived as lacking meaning, then it will block your creativity.

3. The Deadline

For the third and most well-known form of stress and time pressure – the deadline – I defer again to Teresa Amabile. In her previously mentioned book, *The Progress Principle*, she studies seven creative teams from three different sectors and tries to ascertain how much deadlines impede or enhance creativity.

During the first setting, employees had a tight deadline and were carrying out 'treadmill'-work of little importance under high pressure. Their efforts bore little significance, so they lacked motivation to start thinking creatively about their work. They primarily had to deal with ad-hoc tasks and "extinguishing fires," which kept them busy but didn't bring them closer to finishing their core business.

Very long deadlines also had a negative influence on creative thinking. This was especially true when employees "disappeared" in large project teams, spent most of their time assisting others, or spent too much time on the same assignment.

Employees who had to deal with moderate deadlines – that kept the middle between the two mentioned above – or even with tight deadlines, but in that case with a meaningful task that benefited their core business, performed significantly better when it came to creativity.

The stress of a deadline may not always be fun but it forces you to focus on your assignment and prevents you from getting distracted. People are willing to accept a deadline and work towards a creative solution as long as they keep thinking that this deadline is meaningful too and helps to accomplish the core business tasks.

The best way to make those creative juices flow is Italian coffee and a killing deadline.

LEARNINGS & IDEAS

This is your free space to reflect on what the previous story might have taught you and how you can use this knowledge in your own (work) environment. Let the questions here below stimulate you, take a pen and start writing!

- How can you enhance your time management to maximise your (or your team's) creativity?
- Can you transform 'auto-pilot' tasks into 'mission' tasks to stimulate your (or your team's) creativity?
- For your next project, can you try to (better) balance your (or your team's) deadlines, so they become 'moderate'?

Cyril Parkinson was a British ship's historian who spent a great deal of his life in the British civil service. As a British staff officer in the Second World War, he saw how an excess of bureaucracy caused a lot of inefficiency. He noticed, for instance, that the British Colonial Office grew year after year whereas the British Empire was shrinking. In a satirical article in the Economist in 1955, he wrote how organizations seemed to grow uncontrollably because of their selfish nature. The punch line for his essay was: **"Work expands to fill the time available for its completion."** Later he would work this idea into the book that we know as Parkinson's Law. Nowadays, his supposition may be even more on the money than at the time he wrote it over 50 years ago.

PARKINSON'S LAW

We will always **fill up** the space we are **given**

Parkinson's Law may have been inspired by the consequences of a too-large bureaucracy, but it applies to almost everything we do. A few examples:

- **Time:** The closer to the deadline you start with a task, the more productive you are. You get a lot more done in that 'last hour' than at any other time.

- **Space:** Regardless of how much space you have, your belongings will always find a way to use it up. Without realizing it, you acquire more possessions to fill your unused space.

- **Stock:** Most people will eat everything that's on their plate even though they became full long before. Putting less on your plate or eating from smaller plates is therefore common diet advice.

- **Money:** People who earn a lot of money will often spend more too. They buy more things or more expensive things even though they don't really need those things.

That's why I would like to apply his supposition to a broader context and assert: **"We will always, in one way or another, fill up the space we are given."** In other words, people will always use the time, space, budget or means they have at hand. And 'use' doesn't necessarily mean efficiently utilized or delivering a better end result. An excess of time will hardly ever make a work of art – whether it be a book, a painting or a theatre play – more powerful or more interesting. A house with 25 rooms will not always contribute to the comfort of its inhabitants, let alone enhance the coziness. Someone with a monthly salary of € 10.000 is not necessarily happier than their neighbour who earns only € 2.000 despite the fact that the former may have significantly more material possessions.

And of course you can't expand your limitations endlessly. There comes a time where that just doesn't work anymore. You can't write a valuable book in one day any more than you can live comfortably and without a care in the world on just €100,- per month in our Western world. Looking for the correct balance between too little and too much is a balancing act that requires a lot of falling down and standing back up.

The urban legend
of Hemingway's
six-word story

How do you tell a story in only six words? Most people will undoubtedly frown at this crazy idea. And although we are now accustomed to expressing messages in few words (think Twitter), this assignment seems a bit absurd.

The inception of the 'six-word-story' legend has been debated profusely for years, but frankly, it doesn't matter. According to lore, it finds its origins with the famous writer Ernest Hemingway. The story goes that at a dinner, Hemingway engaged in a wager with his companions – all of them writers – that he could write a complete story in only six words. The challenge was accepted, and Hemingway wrote the legendary sentence *'For sale, Baby shoes, Never worn.'* on a napkin. He passed the napkin around and collected the money. Or so the tale goes.

True or not, the concept presented in the story is interesting in its own right and poses the question of how far one can go with literary constraints. Nowadays, one can find a great number of Internet communities that have set up websites based on this challenge, with a

Ernest Hemingway. He challenged his friends with the six-word story and came up with the legendary phrase here on the left – at least, according to (urban) legend.

lot of literary gems as a result. It is an exercise that I often do with my trainees and students. You can easily develop other variations on it, like *'design your epitaph in six words'* or *'write a sentence of six words about what creativity is to you'.*

Other variants of the concept are the mini-saga (50 words), twitterature (140 words) and flash fiction (1,000 words). The last variety contains a full narrative and development of characters. You find these mini stories in short literary supplements in magazines.

Are you inspired to write a six-word story yourself? Here are a few tips:

- **Get inspired** by what others have done before you. As stated before, there are many communities online where you can sometimes find great examples. For example, you can start at www.sixwordstories.net.

- Your story doesn't need to have a beginning, a middle, and an end like a classical story. However, **it does need a plot** to make the reader use their imagination.

- Use **at least one verb** because verbs lead to action. Something 'happens'. Because if nothing happens, it is just a statement, and not really a story.

- Go for the **twist** or the **contradiction**. You only have six words, so you have to be surprising. Say what the reader doesn't expect or employ some **mystery**.

- Use **punctuation**. Periods, commas, colons, question marks, quotation marks, etc. This way you can split up your story into two or more sentences and say more. It also gives rhythm to your story.

12x6 TO FRAME

BROKEN WINGS TWITCH. STRUGGLE. GASP... SILENCE.

I tried, he died, I'm sorry.

Harold died one minute too late.

Sometimes you win, sometimes you learn.

And suddenly we were strangers. Again.

"COME." "OVER MY DEAD BODY." "DOABLE."

Realizing I deserved better changed everything.

I'll meet you where we began.

Love me forever. Then return home.

She met her soulmate. I didn't.

Mom taught me how to shave.

SORRY SOLDIER, SHOES SOLD IN PAIRS.

WHEN
EACH CM³
COUNTS

Reduce to the max and use to the full

The human population of our planet keeps growing, but Planet Earth is not extendable. How do we travel, live, and feed ourselves on a planet with finite resources? These questions are at the heart of many reflections, and innovative solutions are not lacking.

When the box becomes a caravan

For those who are torn between the desire to vacation in a caravan and the fear of quickly becoming irritated by the limitations created by the vehicle, there is Tipoon. Tipoon is an ultra-compact caravan. At first glance it looks like a trailer covered with a roof, but with a button on a remote control this box unfolds and is transformed into a caravan that is 20 m^3 wide and 1,90 meters high, for 10 m^2 of total area.

The space has been ingeniously equipped with room for storage, a water source, a kitchen, and two double beds. Four people can travel there comfortably. Tipoon designers also made the vehicle energy efficient: it was designed not to resist wind, which reduces the fuel consumption of the towing vehicle. Created in 2018, the Tipoon caravan is sold for ±€ 24.000.

The Tipoon is a small but fully equipped caravan

When sleeping becomes too expensive

In densely populated cities, finding accommodations can be a real headache for both tourists and locals. On the one hand, there isn't a lot of free space for apartments, hotels, or other accommodations. On the other hand, the space that is available is usually very expensive. One innovative option for residents and curious tourists in Japan are capsule hotels. People who need a solution (and are not light sleepers) for low-cost accommodations can opt for these dormitory spaces in which tiny private areas are installed. Each contains a bed, a television and Wi-Fi. The capsules are closed either by a porthole or by an airtight curtain, and personal belongings can be stored in secure lockers. Guests share common areas like bathrooms and kitchens. There are also modern capsule hotels that combine business with pleasure and are trendy and comfortable.

The Japanese capsule hotels come in different forms and sizes

Empty wallet geeks may be more attracted to manga kissa. Manga are Japanese comic books, and kissa are tea houses, so a manga kissa is a kind of private library. You pay by the hour to sit and read comic books, while having the option of indulging in various refreshments. These places are generally identifiable via large colored signs, and offer mangas, magazines and DVDs that can be used in cabins equipped with computers and Wi-Fi. For a few thousand yen, you can relax for a few hours and even spend the night! There's no bed, but you can get a reasonable night's sleep on the chair, or there's usually just about enough room to stretch out on the floor. Some manga kissa also have shower rooms and all of them include a bar where guests can enjoy free drinks.

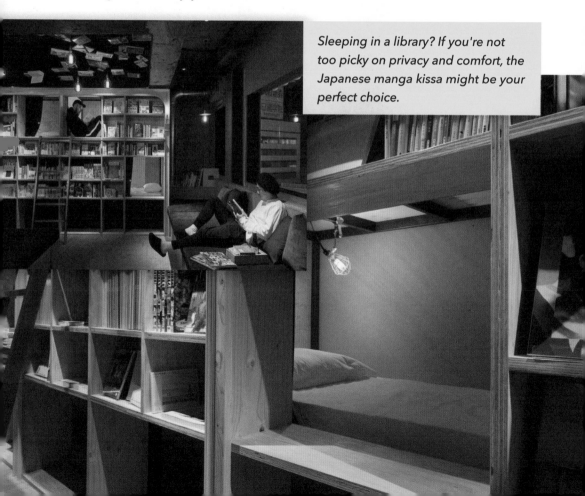

Sleeping in a library? If you're not too picky on privacy and comfort, the Japanese manga kissa might be your perfect choice.

When the fields are missing

In 1999, Dickson Despommier, professor of public health and microbiology at Columbia University, challenged his students: the number of mouths to feed will not stop growing. How can we ensure there will be enough for all to survive? According to the professor, if nothing changes, it will be necessary to find the equivalent of the surface of Canada in new farmland, which is impossible unless we decide to clearcut the forests to replace them with fields.

You can easily imagine the terrible effects such a decision would have on biodiversity and the environment. This question joined that of the quality of life in megacities and big cities. These are becoming more populated. Columbia students developed the urban agriculture framework and calculated the available farmland on the rooftops of New York. This space, if used for food, could feed only 2% of the Big Apple's population. Moving agriculture into the cities is on the right track. Dickson Despommier then suggested to his students to think "out of the field" and move production inside the buildings. Thus, the concept of vertical farming was born.

AeroFarms in Newark is one of the most publicized companies in vertcal farming.

It is found in North America, today, but also in Asia and Europe. The most publicized company is probably AeroFarms. Located in Newark, New Jersey, they grow arugula, watercress or kale. Rather than being buried in the ground, the roots of the plants are set up high, on racks. They hang and are sprinkled with water and nutrients. According to Aero Farms' designers, this growing system - called aeroponics - makes it possible to use 95% less water than conventional agriculture, but also very little fertilizer and no pesticides. Furthermore, the return is constant throughout the year, regardless of the season.

Another advantage: production is local and is sold locally. This avoids the ecological costs of transporting food. Also, it's easy to install the production in abandoned or unoccupied buildings. The most commonly cited disadvantage of vertical agriculture? Electrical consumption, as plants and vegetables do not get the benefit of daylight. While it's still too early to confirm the profitability and sustainability of these vertical farms, they are undeniably part of a wave of innovative and creative solutions for bringing agriculture back to the city.

There are many citizens and companies who embark on the adventure of rooftop farms, urban gardens, shared gardens. In Romainville, France, at the moment, people are working on building the first market gardening city. It will include a glass tower 20 meters high dedicated to the production of fruits and vegetables, but also educational gardens, a restaurant and a point of sale for products grown in the tower. Ideas and initiatives that may seem a bit far-fetched are often effective.

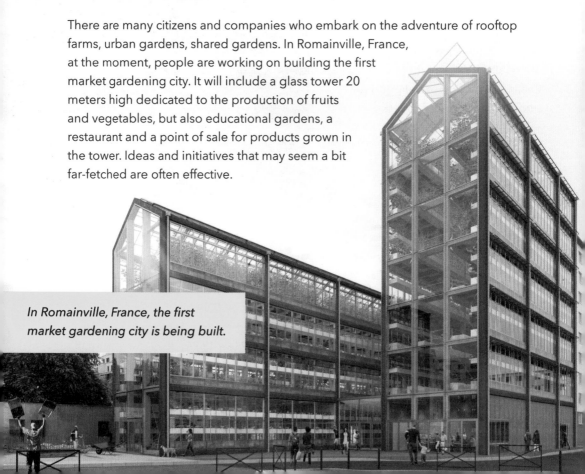

In Romainville, France, the first market gardening city is being built.

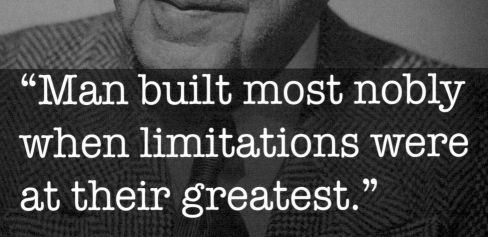

"Man built most nobly when limitations were at their greatest."

Frank Lloyd Wright
American architect and interior designer

LONDON
CALLING
TO THE
FARAWAY
TIMES

When the **box** is **obsolete**

Creative uses of old London phone booths

When you think of renowned cities, a few images always come to mind. When you hear Paris, you see the Eiffel Tower, the Arch of Triumph, and a man wearing a beret on his head with a baguette under his arm. New York is very different, with its cosmopolitan character, towering skyscrapers, hustle and bustle, the dampness rising from the street vents, and the Statue of Liberty. London is visually associated with Big Ben, the Tower Bridge, the double-decker buses, its taxis, and, of course, the ubiquitous red phone booths…

Huh, phone booths? Are they still in use? Are they even still there? Yes, although most have lost their original function. The first units date back to the early 1920s and they became part of the cityscape in no time. The red color was used to stand out and attract attention when people were trying to find a telephone urgently. Over the years, the booths have had makeovers but the design has largely been maintained.

Without its iconic phone booths, London wouldn't be London anymore. But how to preserve them within the cityscape? Leave it to the Brits to solve the challenge of maintaining them with functionality and creativity! On the next pages you'll find four striking examples.

Smartphone **Repair Shop**

The British company Lovefone has transformed the old London phone booths into the smallest of repair shops. And what else would you repair in a phone booth but… phones? The booths' exteriors are kept completely intact, while inside the cell there is room for only one repair man. *'We wanted to create an environment that wouldn't look stuffed, despite all the equipment, tools, and spare parts that had to be kept at hand.',* says designer Giles Gilbert Scott, *'We have kept the windows free, so everyone can have a peek inside.'*

The Solarbox

An empty battery is a common problem for smartphone users. And that inspired Harold Craston and Kirsty Kenney, two student entrepreneurs, to try their hand at rekindling the iconic phone booths. According to the inventors, the Solarbox – which takes its power from solar panels fitted on the roof of the phone booth – can charge approximately 100 phones per day. Inside the box, you'll find different chargers fitting most smartphones. The service is completely free of charge and financed by the commercials shown to users as they charge their phones.

Salad Bar

In Bloomsbury Square, a park in the center of London, you'll find Spier's Salads. Like many London salad bars, he sells salads that are made only with organic, locally sourced ingredients. This wouldn't be anything new, except that he runs his salad bar out of an authentic London phone booth. Spier makes all the salads at home and brings them to his salad bar in Bloomsbury Square. *'I have always had a thing for these beautiful phone booths,'* he says, *'so this way I contribute to not letting them disappear from the cityscape.'*

London's smallest library

Lending a book is not a new thing in itself, but it is when it's done from a London phone booth. 'It's not what you get, it's what you leave behind' is the philosophy that the inventor of this swapping library left behind. People can borrow books from the libraries and leave their old books for others to borrow. Sebastian Handley, who created the concept, spent £500 to renovate the phone booth. The micro-library is now being touted as London's smallest library, with approximately 200 titles ranging from autobiographies to fiction and guides. There is even a shelf for children's books so that the smallest citizens can also visit this mini library.

WHEN WIND
AND COLD
FIRE UP YOUR
CREATIVITY

Polar explorer Dixie Dansercoer **embraces the limitations** the elements impose

'No, I'm not looking for extreme situations per se, and I'm even less of a polar bear that only gets fired up at temperatures under -25°C,' says Dixie Dansercoer, the Belgian polar explorer sitting in front of me. Dansercoer has many miles to his name and is already 55 years old, but his youthful zeal and drive mask his age. I have known him for years as a man with tremendous positive energy, but also a mellowness you wouldn't associate with a rugged adventurer. *'It's the drive to discover things for yourself that must prevail. So, no, not adrenaline or self-flagellation, but indomitable curiosity is what drives me.'*

As a tween, he left for America with only 200 dollars in his pocket to chase the dream: wave-riding and kite surfing on the waves of Hawaii's beaches. He worked underpaid hospitality jobs to survive and practiced hard to improve his skills. After some time, he even won the Belgian championship. *'But that was only the beginning. I knew I was fated to travel, to go places no-one had ever gone before. Only then would I find peace within myself.'* Today, his laurels are impressive, as is his ever growing commitment to the protection of our planet.

Dixie Dansercoer: "'You'll never get anywhere when you consider the elements your enemy. You can't fight them, so you have to accept them. Even more so, you have to learn to embrace them."

His primary professional focus lies in the Polar Regions (North and South Poles), where the wind and cold reign supreme. *'You'll never get anywhere when you consider the elements your enemy'*, says Dixie, *'You can't fight them, so you have to accept them. Even more so, you have to learn to embrace them. And then it becomes interesting because then you can reconcile yourself with their supremacy and find the peace to work your magic from.'* Peace and quiet are words Dixie often uses. *'We have lost something along the way, and that's a pity. To be able to empty your head and from there obtain new perspectives, find creative solutions. It's an incredible luxury if you're able to do that.'*

Looking for the wind

His former experience as a kite surfer gave Dixie the idea to use kites on his polar expeditions. *'Where on foot without any equipment you can go only 30 kilometers in a day at the most, a kite takes you 250 kilometers onwards easily.'* In the beginning, Dixie built his own kites, but it wasn't easy to find the right materials that were both light and strong. *'Weight is crucial to us polar explorers. Every ounce we lose we win because you're towing a sled of more than 185 kilograms when you're out on an expedition for more than 100 days. And under very harsh conditions upon that.'*

Only later he found out that NASA was also developing a kite, be it for a very different reason. The NASA Wing was intended to enable shuttles to land on Earth. They therefore needed a high capacity for braking. Dixie reversed their construction, converting their high breaking power into a pulling force by drawing more propulsive force from the wind. It is a beautiful combination of interdisciplinary and inverted creative thinking.

But what do you do when not a leaf is turning, not a feather is being ruffled? Dixie is not big on accepting the status quo, so he went looking for solutions. *'When the wind doesn't find you, you have to go find the wind yourself,'* he says facetiously.

Dixie Dansercoer: 'When the wind doesn't find you, you have to go find the wind yourself'

'There is always wind, we just don't always feel it because we operate on the ice, where we're right in the middle of a friction zone that lowers minimal wind even more. Why are modern windmills being built so high? Because the wind is that high, so we have to get those kites up as high as possible.' Using extra-long ropes, he launched the kites as high as 100 meters. That's four times their usual height. But there was an additional challenge: how do we get that kite that high into the air on zero-wind-days? *'Take a look at children on the beach. What do they do to get their wind kite high up in the air? They run to get speed and thus use the apparent wind! The solution, therefore, is to use standing practices and convert them to our situation.'*

The minimal weight of the new kites – they are now "single-foil" to avoid the development of heavy air chambers – allows modern polar explorers to bring several models with them. And that means they have a kite available for every wind-speed.

Stay dry and agile

As an ambassador for the Polar Regions, Dixie is very concerned with the climate: *'Global warming has caused the polar caps to melt, leading to more open water that breaks up ice fields. Those zones force us to make detours of many kilometers to retrace a junction to the relatively straight line of our destination. To avoid that, we prefer to cross the water.'* But that is not without peril. In addition to unpredictable currents that

Dixie Dansercoer: "Global warming has caused the polar caps to melt, leading to more open water that breaks up ice fields."

can drag you away, you don't want to get soaked with icy water because it takes a few days for everything to dry, especially with all the salt that your clothes absorb. For this reason, a waterproof suit is the best solution. They are common in the boating industry, but they are not tailored to the specific circumstances of the Polar Regions. They are too thick, too heavy, too cumbersome…

'*A suit like that needs to be fairly sturdy,*' Dixie continues, '*because you have to break with your body the chunks of ice you encounter in the water.*' He joined forces with textile manufacturer Sioen and designed a suit to meet those specific needs. First, there was the weight. The target was to stay below one kilogram without compromising on sturdiness, including extra pads for damage-prone areas like knees, backside, and soles. Agility was also a prerequisite: the suit had to be donned over already bulky thermic wear and not in the most comfortable of circumstances.

'*Also, it had to be compatible with ski materials, so we looked for a simple click-on system, making it possible to keep using skis easily.*', Dixie recounts.

That the suit had to be water proof was clear from the beginning. '*But you don't want to be inside a plastic bag.*' Dixie explains, '*Wading through water is rather straining, making you perspire easily.*' He decided to use the well-known 'Immersion' Goretex fabric, which allows for moist body warmth to go from the inside to the outside, but at the same time blocks moisture from coming in.

'*Of course, we're talking about a very exclusive suit that is used under very specific circumstances. A suit like that you're not going to produce for the mass market, because the number of polar explorers in the world you can easily count on two hands,*' Dixie laughs. The fruits of this kind of extraordinary designs you will only reap success with the innovation of products for a larger market. For the manufacturer, Dixie's extreme operational circumstances are a fortunate form of field R&D with a clear win-win as a result.

You want to go on a polar expedition with Dixie Dansercoer? www.polarcircles.com

When the **box** has to fit the **tube**

How creativity saved three astronauts

On 13 April 1970, on the third manned mission to the moon, one of the Apollo 13's two oxygen tanks exploded. Unexpectedly, astronauts Lovell, Swigert, and Haise had to abort their mission and were forced to return to earth. Not a walk in the park, because their vessel was badly damaged. The legendary words 'Houston, we have a problem' find their origin here. In its 60 years of existence, NASA has put men on the moon and robots on Mars. But maybe this was the biggest 'tour de force' in its history: saving the lives of the three stranded astronauts 300,000 kilometers from Earth. It was a show of creative thinking with two real constraints as the challenge: time and means.

All non-essential systems were shut down to save energy. The astronauts moved to the lunar module that had enough means for two men for two days. Now those means would have to last long enough for three men for four days. There was enough oxygen on board, but energy and water had to be rationed. And carbon dioxide build-up would most likely prove to be the biggest problem. That's why Mission Control worked on the filter problem. The containers with lithium hydroxide that were used to filter the carbon dioxide in the lunar module were tubular shaped, while the available containers in the mission module were cubically shaped.

How do you fit a round tube into a square box? That was the assignment put before the three astronauts. The materials they had on board were very limited, and the clock was ticking because with every minute the level of nitrogen rose significantly. Ground control took over, and a number of engineers tackled the problem. They didn't solve this problem through discussion or by making complicated calculations on paper, but by using some good old elbow grease and building a prototype.

They made a list of all materials aboard the lunar module, collected them rapidly, and spread them out on a table. The filters were represented by a cardboard box and a plastic tube. They needed only a few minutes to come up with the solution: an apparatus constructed of duct tape, spare parts from space suits, and tube socks. Jokingly, they called the prototype 'the mailbox'. It wasn't really an example of refined technique or aesthetics, but it worked.

The construction of the "mailbox" was communicated to the astronauts, and miraculously, they managed to copy it precisely. The tube was connected to the box and in no time at all the nitrogen level dropped. Mission succeeded. Three days later, Apollo 13 landed safely back on earth.

Picture on top: the crew of Apollo 13.

Picture on the right: the 'mailbox' solution that saved the astronauts.

LEARNINGS & IDEAS

This is your free space to reflect on what the previous story might have taught you and how you can use this knowledge in your own (work) environment. Let the questions here below stimulate you, take a pen and start writing!

- How well is your organisation prepared to come up with creative solutions in unforeseen situations that restrain your possibilities?
- Are you or your people well trained and flexible/cool enough to come up with great solutions in that case? And do you have the supporting processes and tools for it?

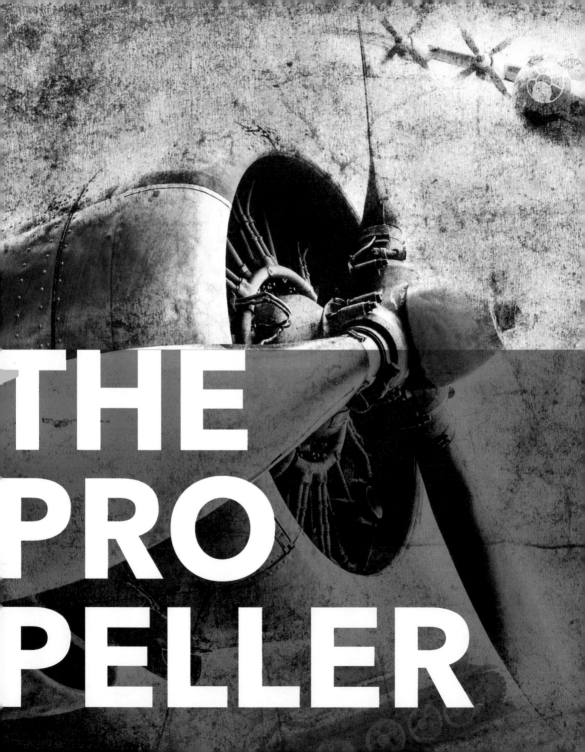

THE
PRO
PELLER

Fly Higher, Dig Deeper: **The Propeller**

TECHNIQUE IN BRIEF ON PAGE 182

Why is it that it's so much easier for us to come up with solutions and answers for other people's problems than for our own ones? Is it because we're initially lazy, well aware of the answer to our problem but ignoring it, so we don't have to face the effort the solution requests? Perhaps it is, in some cases at least. Giving instructions is much more comfortable than getting the work done yourself, isn't it? Or is it that giving advice is somehow cheap and without consequences? True, because if it turns out bad, we don't have to pay the price for it. It was not our problem, to begin with. Yes, that certainly plays a role in our heroic daring to others and our silent cowardice to ourselves.

But there might be another reason as well: we often simply don't see the solution, because we're blinded by the constraints that seem inevitable to us. It's like we're in a maze and can't find our way out because we're standing in the middle of it. In such a case, we actually need to be lifted up from the maze to see all of the the obstacles that keep us from reaching the exit.

That's exactly what The Propeller will do: give you an overview to not only see the obstacles but also find your way out. First, you outline the challenge. Secondly, you identify the constraint that blocks you from finding a satisfactory solution. And thirdly, you ask the question why it is a constraint and what it exactly impedes. Great if you can find an answer to that and even greater if you can overcome the obstacle by finding an alternative solution. If not, dig deeper, ask yourself the why-question again and again. And with each answer may come a better solution. That's how it works. But there's more. The Propeller also stimulates you to finetune your ideas and translate them into real and applicable solutions.

You can apply this technique all by yourself, but like many other techniques, it's way more fun and much more rewarding to do this in a group. You can download the PDF-file of the graph free of charge at www.whentheboxisthelimit.com/propeller or scan the QR-code on the left.

How it works:

STEP 1

- Print the graph in a large size, minimum A2, but bigger is better, certainly when you work in a group.

- Put the graph on the table or hang it on the wall. See what works best for you / your team.

- Provide post-its to everyone, preferably small ones that will fit into the blue and green boxes on the graph.

STEP 2

- Discuss the central question or problem and make sure that everyone understands it clearly. Write the question down if necessary and keep it visible during the entire process.

- Take a large post-it note and write down the constraint. Define it concisely and clearly, and stick it in the dark blue area in the middle of the propeller graph.

- Limit yourself to one constraint at a time. If there are more, you can go through the process again

at a later stage or use a second graph simultaneously, that may be handled by another team where relevant, appropriate or necessary.

STEP 3

- Try to describe why it is a constraint. There can be more than one reason, and that's why the graph foresees three 'A' areas around the central constraint. I recommend you use all three of them.

- Write the restriction caused by the constraint(s) on (a) small post-it note(s) and stick them in the clear blue areas marked 'A'.

STEP 4

- Now it's time to come up with alternatives. How can you overcome this constraint? How can this issue be solved differently? Be creative and come up with an original idea for each constraint defined 'A'.

- Use your imagination. In this stage of the process, don't be too harsh on yourself or others if the idea is not quite realistic yet.

- Stick the idea on the green areas marked 'A1'.

STEP 4+

- *You can do STEP 4+ later and continue with STEP 5, or you can decide to go for this challenge straight away.*

- *Try to enhance the feasibility of the alternative idea you came up with in 'A1' as much as possible. Build on the basic form of the idea, try to finetune it, and ask yourself 'how could it really work?'*

- *As this is a process, stick your first ideas on the 'A2' area, and continue to stick subsequent ideas to increase the feasibility into the other areas 'A3', 'A4' and 'A5' that lead to the periphery of the graph.*

STEP 5

- *We have defined why the main constraint restricts us in STEP 3 (in the 'A' area). But there might be a more 'underlying' or primary obstacle. We want to dig deeper.*

- *Based on the defined restriction, we ask ourselves again 'why is this a restriction?' The answer to that question, we write down on a small post-it note and stick it in area 'B'. And we do so for all three 'B' areas.*

STEP 6

- *This is a duplication of STEP 4, except that we're now talking about the constraints stuck in the 'B' areas. Follow the same instructions as in STEP 4 and replace 'A' with 'B'.*

- *Stick the ideas onto the green areas marked 'B1'.*

STEP 6+

- *This is a duplication of STEP 4+, except that we're now talking about the alternative solution stuck in the 'B1' area. So follow the same instructions as in STEP 4+ and replace 'A1' through 'A5' with 'B1' through 'B4'.*

STEP 7

- *The same scenario repeats itself, always digging deeper, until you reach the 'E' areas.*

AND WHAT IF YOU JUST LEAVE OUT THE GIST?

Radical constraints
beget radical innovation

Will your company still exist in 10 years or more? How long can you keep doing what you are doing today? And how relevant will your activity still be knowing that the world is changing at an exponential rate? Many companies and organizations hardly dare to ask themselves these existential questions. And yet we are consumed with innovation. We keep a close eye on our market, we know exactly what our competition is doing, we know our customers like the back of our hand, and we even have a genuine R&D team continuously looking at our services and products and adjusting them where necessary.

Adjusting? Is that innovating? Well, for the majority of organizations and companies that's what it means. A little polishing here and there, a fresh color or a mild adjustment of our service model. Why would we do more than that? The client doesn't ask for it, do they? Right… and maybe that is one of the main reasons why we like to be careful. Moreover, radical innovation brings a lot of risk with it. And we don't want that. We prefer to go slowly. Disruptive innovation is for the big league guys because they can afford to financially. Or for start-ups because they have nothing to lose yet.

"If I had asked people what they wanted, they would have said faster horses." This is a famous quote from Henry Ford. On the one hand, it explains that improving existing products or services are not always the route to disruptive innovation. On the other hand, it emphasizes that innovation may never spring from clients' wishes. The client may be king, yet he very rarely is a visionary.

The automobile is indeed a textbook example of radical innovation. What Ford basically did is leave out the gist. This is also what you find in the ideas behind many other radical innovations. It is the most extreme constraint you can impose on yourself as an innovator. The question behind it that Ford – consciously or subconsciously – asked himself may have been: 'How do I make a (horse) carriage WITHOUT horses?' Below you'll find a number of other examples that have brought about radical changes with the same kind of constraining core question behind the innovations.

A shop without shop space

When the Internet was still in its infancy in the early 1990s, many creative young entrepreneurs grabbed their chance to come up with totally new business models to disrupt the existing market. Among them was Jeff Bezos, who founded **Amazon** in 1994. Originally focused on the sale of books, the range of products on offer in the online store grew extensively in just a few years. Today there are hardly any products you can't find on Amazon, and Bezos was named the richest man on earth in 2017.

A vacuum cleaner without dust bag

 If you randomly asked someone 20 years ago to name the five essential features of a vacuum cleaner, the dust bag undoubtedly would have been one of them. In 1978, James **Dyson** was frustrated by the decreasing performance of his vacuum

cleaner. He took the machine apart and noticed that the
dust bag was clogged with dust impeding the suction.
'I discovered what was going wrong with dust bags
and thought of something more efficient. That
is the beauty of sustainable designs and
the gist of them: 'do more with less',
according to James Dyson.

A fan without blades

Next to the famous bag-less
vacuum cleaner, you will also find
the 'less is more'
philosophy in other
products by **Dyson**.
When you think 'fan,' you immediately see rotating blades in
your head. They are the hypostasis of the product itself. And yet,
James Dyson managed to make a perfect working fan without
blades. That this innovation is not only original and creative, but
also effective is proven by the higher ventilation power, the lower
power use, and the reduction of noise that the fan produces. Less is
more indeed.

dyson

CIRQUE DU SOLEIL°

A circus without animals

For the past few decades, the classical circus was waning in popularity. Add to that the increasing protests against the use (or abuse) of animals during the shows, and it's easy to see that the formula didn't work anymore. Two Canadian street artists thought this way too, and they created **Cirque du Soleil**, a concept for a circus without animals, but with even more daring acrobats, extravagant costumes, and music to go with it. The idea gained traction, and the rest is history. With exotic names like Saltimbanco, Alegria or Zarkana, the circus draws millions of spectators worldwide and employs over 5000 people today.

A hotel chain without hotels

If there is one company that has disrupted the travel industry, it's **Airbnb**. Founded in 2008 by three young entrepreneurs, it was noticed by investors only after a weak start and was eventually professionalized. Today, the website contains more than 3 million private accommodations in 192 countries and 33,000 cities and is – despite the controversy it causes with cities, locals, and the classic hotel industry alike - estimated to be worth $25 billion. This value makes it the most successful 'hotel chain' worldwide.

A taxi company without vehicles

Uber is often mentioned in the same breath as Airbnb. And that's not surprising because the concepts have a lot in common. Both are about mobility, calling on 'ordinary' citizens instead of schooled professionals, and disrupting a whole industry (admittedly including the necessary troubles). And similar to what happened with Airbnb, once again, out of an extreme constraint a gigantic corporation grew. You can be friend or foe of the concepts, but the fact is that Uber, as well as Airbnb, brought about radical changes that sparked the innovation motors in both industries tremendously.

"If I had asked people what they wanted, they would have said faster horses."

Henry Ford

LEARNINGS & IDEAS

This is your free space to reflect on what the previous story might have taught you and how you can use this knowledge in your own (work) environment. Let the questions here below stimulate you, take a pen and start writing!

- Do you have the guts or start-up mentality to disrupt the market?
- Can you leave out the gist to come up with radical new ideas?
- Can you ignore the client's wishes for once and go to the essence of your product or service?
- What about organising a competition for the most radical ideas?

Team work
+ Competition
+ Restrictions

= Creativity³

'Angels and Devils' is a standing exercise I use at every training in creative thinking. It goes like this:

- Divide your group of participants into two teams of 3-5 members.

- One team you call **'Angels'** and the other **'Devils'.**

- Make sure you have at least four participants (more is better) who are ot part of either team. This group is called **'Earthlings.'** They do not constitute a team. Instead, they each work individually.

- Prepare two flip charts with two columns each. In the columns, write **the letters of the alphabet** (on the left from A through M vertically, on the right N through Z) and leave enough space behind each letter to fill in a word. Hang both flip charts on the wall – a bit separated – and ask the groups 'Angels' and 'Devils' to each sit in front of one of the flip charts.

- Give each group a separate assignment (best prepared in advance).

  - **Assignment for the 'Angels':** think up **26 terms of endearment** each starting with a different letter of the alphabet. The group gets 1 marker.

"Never have I encountered the situation where one of the individual 'Earthlings' raises their hand first. It's the teams who take all the glory. "

- *Assignment for the 'Devils':* think up *26 expletives* each starting with a different letter of the alphabet. The group gets 1 marker.

- *Assignment for the 'Earthlings':* think up *26 terms of endearment* or *expletives*, without enforcing any form of restriction. As said before the 'Earthlings' work individually. They remain in their seat and write on their own piece of paper.

- Let all three groups start at the same time and make it clear that the activity is a competition. *Whoever raises their hand first wins!*

Never have I encountered the situation where one of the individual 'Earthlings' raises their hand first. It's the teams who take all the glory. Often, the 'Earthlings' haven't even thought of half of the words requested. The results from the teams are also almost always more original and daring, resulting from the social pressure to be as 'funny' and creative as possible.

You can partly attribute teams consistently finishing before individuals to the fact that there are more people working on the teams. That is partly true, but the element of competition certainly also comes into play. This causes the necessary time pressure, which means the suggestions are hardly evaluated. It's *'anything goes, as long as we complete the flip chart first,'* meaning that the assessment of answers is only based on quantity, not quality. The controversial part of this line of reasoning is that because of the time pressure the quality (read: creativity) rises sugnificantly.

A third factor that increases the flow of creative juices in this exercise is the enforced structure: all 26 letters of the alphabet have to be used as an initial letter. Most participants sigh at this restriction at the beginning, but after only a few seconds it proves to be a stimulant. You'll notice that the letters get used in order of difficulty: the easiest first... and then, in the end, they're left with Q, X, and Y. At the last three, usually, a 'force-to-fit' method is used which results in very creative finds.

In short, teamwork, competition, and enforcing a certain restrictive structure are the three basic ingredients here for generating creative ideas fast.

THE CASUAL CON STRAINT CONTEST

The Casual Constraint Contest

TECHNIQUE IN BRIEF ON PAGE 183

A highly activating team game to generate stunning ideas based on random restrictions

As stated in the previous exercise *'Angels and Devils'*, the combination of team work, competition, and restrictions has a proven track record of being the winning mix to conjure up surprising ideas. That's why I developed the creative game *'The Casual Constraint Contest'*.

The constraints in this game are of a miscellaneous nature and will present themselves very rarely. And that's exactly the point; in real life chances are small these restrictions will come your way and thus will force you to find creative solutions you would have never thought of before. The fact that it's a team process only intensifies your engagement and the urge to come up with surprising ideas, whereas the competition factor adds rhythm and fun to the game.

What you need is:

- a challenge (for instance: how can we improve our product or service? / how do we create a unique brand for our organization? / …)
- a team of at least 6 people
- the tools that come with this game, downlaoadable at www.whentheboxisthelimit.com/casualconstraintcontest Alternatively, you can scan the QR-code on the left
- preferably at least 1 to 1,5 hours of time
- a clear, unstressed, and open mindset of each team member

You can play the game independently from any other creativity stimulating technique, or you can make it part of a brainstorm session and add it as a technique in the divergent phase of your process. As the ideas coming out of The Casual Constraint Contest might be quite revolutionary, I recommend the latter so as to have a proper balance between incremental and disruptive ideas.

How it works:

STEP 1

- Print the tools you downloaded previously, preferably on paper of at least 170 gr/m².

- Let the participants sit around a table. Preferably at least 6 people and when there are more, preferably a multiple of three (9, 12, 15, …).

- Cut the constraint cards (What If Cards.pdf), shuffle them and put them in the middle of the table, blank side up.*

- Cut the sheet with the yellow, red and blue pawn cards (What if Colors.pdf) and let each participant pick one card blindly.* Ideally, the number of colors are equally distributed among the participants (that's why we need a multiple of three participants).

- Cut and assemble the color die (What If Dice.pdf).*

- Provide pens and post-its. Foresee timers (for instance on a smartphone) for half of the total number of participants.

* You can also play with real pawns and a real color die if you prefer. You can order them from the website: www.whentheboxisthelimit.com

STEP 2

- *Discuss the central question or challenge and ensure that everyone understands it clearly. Write the question on the heading of a flipchart and keep it visible during the entire process.*

STEP 3

- *Now we form teams of two participants each. Therefore, we roll the die.*

- *Depending on the color thrown with the die, the teams will be formed:*

  ORANGE
  - *Team(s) of yellow and red*
  - *Team(s) of blue and blue*

  GREEN
  - *Team(s) of yellow and blue*
  - *Team(s) of red and red*

  PURPLE
  - *Team(s) of blue and red*
  - *Team(s) of yellow and yellow*

  YELLOW, RED or BLUE
  - *Team(s) of yellow and yellow*
  - *Team(s) of red and red*
  - *Team(s) of blue and blue*

STEP 4

- *The purpose of the game is to come up with as many ideas as possible. Per idea, the team gets 1 point.*

- *Each team picks 3 constraint cards from the stack and checks the 'What if' question that is written on each card. Don't start conjuring up ideas yet., wait until the timer is set and starts running.*

- *Each team now gets a maximum of 10 minutes to come up with creative ideas to solve the central question or challenge (written on the flipchart) taking into account each 'What if' question on the constraint cards. Do not combine the three constraints, as it will be too difficult or may even be contradictory. Just treat them separately.*

- *Note that for each separate constraint, the team needs to come up with at least 3 valuable ideas. If not, they will lose 10 points. If the team thinks that they won't be able to think up at least 3 ideas for one or more of the constraint cards, they can put that card back and replace it with a new one from the pile. In that case, they lose 1 minute of time per card. So, for instance, if you replace 2 cards, you get only 8 minutes to come up with creative ideas.*

- *Set the timer to the right number of minutes for each team to start conjuring up ideas. Each idea is written separately on a post-it.*

STEP 5

- *When game time is over for everyone, each team sticks their ideas accompanied by a quick explanation on the flipchart.*

- *The number of ideas is counted, and the points (1 point per idea) are awarded per team. Again: fewer than 3 ideas per constraint card means -10 points.*

- *The points are then divided 50/50 among the two team members.*

- *Now you can start again: new teams are formed, and new constraint cards are drawn. So, back to STEP 3. It is best that you decide in advance how many rounds you want to play. Usually, three rounds are recommended.*

STEP 6

- *After the game is played, each participant shows how many points they have collected. The participant with the highest number of points has won.*

- *The group now decides how many ideas they want to develop into a concept. Ideas can be selected by sticking stickers on the preferred ideas (and the most 'stickered' idea(s) will be developed), or the group can decide to form (small) teams again, with each team picking one idea that they want to work on.*

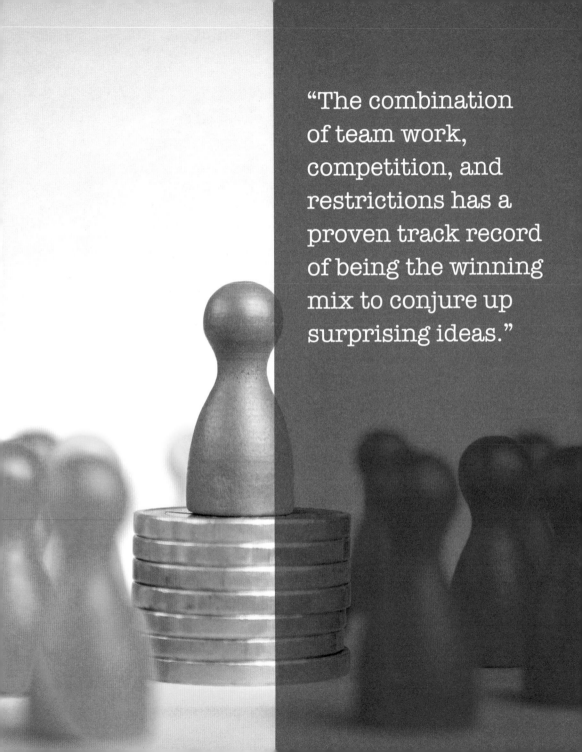

"The combination of team work, competition, and restrictions has a proven track record of being the winning mix to conjure up surprising ideas."

DELICIOUS
DESERT
TOMATOES

Sunlight and Seawater

This is how to grow 17,000 tons of tomatoes annually in a desert

The Oxford Dictionary's definition of the word desert is as follows: *'A waterless, desolate area of land with little or no vegetation, typically one covered with sand.'* Not exactly an apt place for agriculture. The company Sundrops, located at Port Augusta bordering the inhospitable desert of South-Australia, nevertheless manages to grow just about 17,000 tons of tomatoes annually. Yes, really, two loaded trucks a day leave the premises to provide the country with the fresh, healthy and juicy produce.

In 2050, scientists have calculated, 70% more food will be needed to keep feeding the exponentially growing world population. We know that our main sources for producing food - namely energy and water - generated in the classical ways are running out, so we have to find alternatives. That limitations and challenges can't stop innovation is proven by this successful project. The indoor farm of Sundrops – measuring 20 acres – is the first of its sort, and the result of six years of research by an international team of scientists who wanted to find a way to grow crops without the use of fresh water, soil or unnecessary energy from the net. A Sundrops greenhouse transforms seawater and sunlight into fresh water and energy. Next, sustainably produced carbon dioxide and nutrients are used to maximize the crops' growth.

The seawater, used by the Sundrops greenhouse, gets pumped up from the Spencer Gulf five kilometers away and is desalinated on-site by a solar-powered installation. The installation processes it into

A field of 23.000 mirrors reflects the sunlight to a light tower.

fresh (vegetable) water by 'scrubbing' the salt from it. A sensational spectacle employing 23,000 mirrors converges the sunlight into a 'light tower' that does the job *(see image on the opposite page)*. The roots of the vegetables are grown in coconut shells. To cool the plants in the fierce summer heat (temperatures can rise as high as 48 degrees Celsius), the team uses little pieces of cardboard soaked in seawater. The heat of the sun during the summer is enough for the plants to survive the winter months. Another advantage: because the plants are grown in a permanently controlled environment, pesticides are not necessary at all.

Despite the limitations of its natural surroundings, Sundrops succeeds in delivering products of a consistently high quality for a low price in an ecology-proof production environment. Experts are convinced that the Sundrops system can be a solution for the challenges farmers face around the world as fresh water is becoming more scarce, the land is going barren, and energy costs are rising. According to many agricultural scientists, these closed systems that rely on renewable energy are the future of agriculture worldwide.

"According to many agricultural scientists, these closed systems that rely on renewable energy are the future of agriculture worldwide."

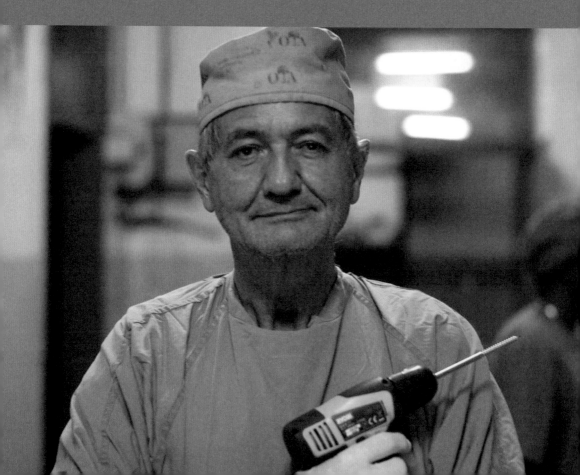

HAND ME THE FISH THREAD, PLEASE!

Surgeon tools straight from the local do-it-yourself shop

'A plumber knows exactly what this is for,' says Erik Erichsen as he shows a clamping ring to connect two tubes, *'but you can treat bone fractures with it perfectly too.'* Erichsen, originally from Sweden, is 70 years old and a driven surgeon. His field of operations is Ethiopia. The tools he works with on a daily basis come from the local do-it-yourself shop.

Do-it-yourself? Yes, because in a country with only three doctors per 100.000 inhabitants where there is no money for expensive surgical tools, you have to make do with the means at hand. *'Look, this is a simple spoke from a bicycle's wheel,'* he continues, *'ideal to perform a bone marrow aspiration and about a thousand times cheaper than its professional pendent.'* That a spoke sometimes is rusty, he accepts. *'Sterile rust is not damaging to the patient,'* he maintains.

Erichsen doesn't have the luxury to send patients to another hospital. He has to address the problem locally with the few means that are at hand. And that requires a great deal of creativity on a regular basis.

Erik and Sennait Erichsen: 'The mental misery in Sweden is much bigger than the physical misery in Ethiopia. We can learn so much from this culture,'

€4,000 for a surgical drill? You have to be crazy to spend that kind of money when the task can be completed just as well with a €25 rechargeable drill. Sewing a wound? Of course, you use nylon fish thread for that!

'The problem is that no one in the so called 'developed world' thinks they can learn anything from Africa. And most certainly not on a medical level,' the surgeon recounts. And yet the creativity and ingenuity of the people who work there top those of the Western world ten times over. Why? Because they have to. That Erichsen is known as the 'rebel surgeon' he laughs off affably: *'I didn't ask to be a rebel. I am not looking for sensationalism or to shock anyone. On the contrary, I have always and everywhere gone out of my way to buy decent hospital material because, of course, it is better to execute such procedures with the equipment that is meant for it. But often there was no money for it. So for lack of better alternatives, in emergency situations, I had to be inventive.'*

In 2017 a documentary named 'The Rebel Surgeon' was made about Erik Erichsen. The surgeon ended up in Africa through his wife Sennait, who is Ethiopian and works in the hospital alongside her husband. When they think of Sweden, it's often with mixed feelings: *'The mental misery in Sweden is much bigger than the physical misery in Ethiopia. We can learn so much from this culture,'* Erichsen concludes.

LEARNINGS & IDEAS

This is your free space to reflect on what the previous story might have taught you and how you can use this knowledge in your own (work) environment. Let the questions here below stimulate you, take a pen and start writing!

- Which expensive products, services, structures, processes, etc. you use in your daily business, can you creatively replace by cheaper alternatives?
- What can you learn from people and organisations in your sector that have to work with less means?

CHEAP, CHEAPER, CHEAPEST

Where **money** is restricted, **creativity** crows victory

An electrical wheelchair for only 500 Euro?
Yes, it can be done!

Unfortunately, not every wheelchair-bound patient can afford an electrical wheelchair. Any e-wheelchair easily costs a few thousand euros, and if you want a better-equipped one, you will be looking at a five-figure number in no time.

A group of students from Brigham Young University were presented with the problem and took the challenge to create an e-wheelchair costing fewer than € 500. After a year of designing, testing, and fine-tuning, they managed to build a model that is suitable for children weighing up to 25 kilograms.

The beauty of this project is that these students have made their plans accessible on the Internet free of charge. Anyone who wants to replicate building the chair can easily do so using the students' clear manuals and effectively doesn't pay more than € 500 in materials, such as frames, motors, batteries, wheels, and electronics facilitating joystick operation. *(www.openwheelchair.org)*

A nice children's wheelchair for under *100 Euro*? Yes, it can be done!

The wheelchair itself is not a new invention. What is new and innovative, however, is marketing a sturdy, fun-looking, and child-friendly wheelchair for under € 100. Business partners Pablo Kaplan and Chava Rothstein gladly took on this challenge with their organization 'Wheelchairs of Hope.' A wheelchair to a child, of course, means loads more than just mobility. In poor countries in particular, it enhances chances at education and social integration significantly and therefore acts as a determining factor for the future chances a child has.

The wheelchair is delivered as a do-it-yourself kit to keep the purchasing price as low as possible. Moreover, the organization also provides a manual for volunteers who help the wheelchair-users to operate the chair correctly. The wheelchair itself is lightweight, agile, and, thanks to the four 'flashy' colors, also attractive for young users.

(www.wheelchairsofhope.org)

A wheelchair for *0 Euro*? Yes, it can be done!

Can it be done still cheaper? Yes, even at no cost at all. But you need 'special' people for that. In the aftermath of a series of civil wars and, subsequently, the collapse of the state in the 1980s and 1990s, the health system of the Democratic Republic of the Congo completely fell apart. A whole generation of Congolese children never received the polio vaccine. These children have since grown up, and the number of handicapped people as a consequence of polio among them is huge. Robert Mboyo unfortunately contracted the disease as a child. His father taught him how to repair bicycles, and Robert used that knowledge to build simple wheelchairs from recycled parts. He provides the wheelchairs free of charge to people who need them but cannot afford them.

To continue this work long-term, in 1997 he started the **'Foundation-Mboyo'** that is financed primarily by donations coming all the way from Europe. People not only donate money, but also spare parts like tires, bolts, and chains. The employees in the organization are often wheelchair-users themselves. *'It's important to support each other because we don't get any help from the government,'* Mboyo explains.

WHEN THE **BOX** IS THE ANSWER

How everyday **cardboard boxes** become inspiring toys or art

On the previous pages we've mainly been talking about making the best of the restricted stuff you find inside the box. In a figurative way that was. Well, let's take it literally for once. And imagine you get a box full of stuff, but nothing inspires you to come up with creative ideas or to find the right way to tackle your challenge. Or it might even be more extreme: the box is empty. There's nothing, nada. Now what?

Well, in that case, all that's left is the box itself. And that simple piece of carton can be quite inspiring to some very creative people. Here are two great examples of how the box became the answer.

Cut-out figures on cardboard relief boxes

Poverty, refugees, disasters… all over the world are people living in gruesome settings. Those people have often a shortage of basic needs like food, medicine and clothing, which – when they're lucky - are sent to them in cardboard relief boxes. Toys for children to play with are not amongst those 'basic needs'. A pity of course, because toys can make a huge difference in a child's life, especially in harsh circumstances.

Lisanne Koning's beautiful concept of using cardboard relief boxes to provide children with colorful cut-out toys.

That's exactly what **Lisanne Koning**, a young Dutch designer, thought as well, and she came up with a great idea. Why not making use of the box itself, which is made out of rigid cardboard, to create some cute drawings children can cut out, assemble and play with?

"There are three different patterns for three different ages", Koning states, *"but the fun thing is that elements from different boxes can be combined with one another."*

All the boxes contain elements from different cultures. This way, children can play with the figures they are familiar with, but also discover other worlds in order to develop their imagination. A very high impact at a very low cost.

A toy store for imaginative kids

Oh yes, there were a few children disappointed when they entered the so-called toy store and didn't perceive any toy. This store was quite a bit different indeed: it only displayed cardboard boxes, and they were all around...

We all know that creativity is one of the most vital talents a child can develop. That was the driving idea behind **Mr Imagine's Toy Store**, a pop-up store that has been set up as part of the **Chicago Children's Museum**. Commercial toys are at first sight very eye-catching and appealing, but they give children often too few imaginative possibilities. With cardboard boxes, it's just the other way around: at first sight they might look a bit dull, but in fact the only limit of a box is the child's imagination. You could say that, although the shop doesn't actually sell any ready-made toy, it sells any toy a child can imagine and create.

The shop included birdhouses, a music area, hot air balloons and even a gigantic castle, all made out of cardboard of course. It also hosted workshops on how to use cardboard to create cool toys. But even technology was present in the form of an augmented reality station where kids could hold up their boxes for some ideas on what kind of toy it could become.

Mr Imagine's Toy Store:
Sorry, only cardboard boxes for sale!

Cardboard Art

The banality that becomes originality: cardboard boxes have also inspired many visual artists, and cardboard art has become a genuine style in the contemporary art scene. When the box becomes a muse, there's some stunning stuff to discover. Here are two of the many examples:

Ana Serrano is a Mexican-American artist who gets inspired from everyday life in the urban neighborhoods of Los Angeles. Traveling throughout the city, she photographs parts of the urban landscape that most of us ignore: such as decorative cast-iron "burglar bars" on a window, a dilapidated but brightly painted door, barbed wire, or the hand-painted signage and illustrations on storefronts. Back at her studio, she uses her photographs, cardboard, and paint to create her own stylized versions of humble icons of urban life, such as a liquor store, a carpet shop, a bakery, or a simple home.

The art of Ana Serrano is entirely made of cardboard and inspired by daily life in Los Angeles.

Using only packaging cardboard and glue, without any supporting structure, wooden or metal frame, **Chris Gilmour** creates striking sculptures. The artist underlines the transposition between the original object and the one made of cardboard. Not only simple copies but rather translations from life, his sculptures bring the knowledge of small things that hide the sense of daily existence. His astonishing life-size sculptures are always grounded on everyday objects we have all experienced in person.

Chris Gilmour's sculptures: Aston Martin DB5 (top left), Olivetti Lettera 22 (bottom left) and Vesperbild (right).

THE BEAUTY
OF UGLINESS

When humor turns a weakness into a virtue

Ugliness is a sacred burden. In many cases, the weapon chosen to evade it is humor. And a nice dose of creativity of course. Because it's not just about evoking a smile, you also have to convince people. Whether it's a city, a hotel, a car or food... some "ugly things" have become successful thanks to the creative ways a few entrepreneurs managed to find their audience.

When ugly is exotic

In 2008, the Dutch newspaper De Volkskrant awarded **Charleroi** (a city in Belgium) the title *"ugliest city in the world"*. This description aroused the curiosity of other international journalists who couldn't really disagree with what their Dutch colleagues wrote. It must be said that with its abandoned industrial sites, shopping streets without businesses, and a gray sky to depress the best of optimistic natures, the Belgian city didn't have a lot going for it.

This inglorious portrait displeased artist Nicolas Buissart. Although wearing pink glasses and denying the reality of his hometown is not his thing, Nicolas decided to offer a different view of the region. He

Picture on the left: The Belgian city of Charleroi was awarded the title 'ugliest city in the world'. With lots of humor and creativity, artist Nicolas Buissart turned this constraint into a real unique advantage.

came to the conclusion that these ugly spots grouped together in such a small place were not an ordinary thing. And what is not ordinary deserves attention. Therefore, Nicolas decided to organize urban safaris. The *"ugliest city in the world"* has become the city that *"offers a wide range of exciting attractions"*. Participants of the Urban Safari have the opportunity to discover, not without humor, the place where the mother of the painter Magritte committed suicide, the "Waste of Time" street described as the most depressing of Belgium, a phantom subway, dilapidated factories, and the abandoned carcass of an old aircraft left on a vacant lot along a national highway. These places seemed repulsive, frightening even. But now they have become areas loaded with mystery, and Charleroi has been stamped the "most interesting post-industrial region of Europe".

Today, we can say that the Vol)skrant article was the trigger and that Nicolas Buissart's initiative set the tone. Even if the face of Charleroi has undergone a first facelift, no one has tried to erase either its character or its history. Examples? Wearing a "Charleroi is the New Black" t-shirt has become trendy, and the best international DJs perform at Rockerill, a collection of old forges left in their original state. Political and cultural parties now understand that being "the ugliest city in the world" was not only a disadvantage.

Making bad reviews your trademark

The owners of the **Hans Brinker Hotel** in Amsterdam are very proud: their hotel is the worst in the world. Their pride is the result of a smart marketing strategy which started from reading the disastrous comments of customers about dirty rooms, noise, rudeness of staff, bathrooms that look

Picture on the right: Posters of the Hans Brinker Hotel in Amsterdam. Bad service, dirty rooms, lack of comfort and other horror... as a USP. ▶

like torture rooms, etc. They could have decided to improve its comfort but, instead, the owners turned to KesselsKramer, a communications agency that helped them to highlight all the faults in the accommodation with funny, sarcastic messages that magnify the tone of the comments. The tone is the same on the website.

The result? Hans Brinker is virtually sold out throughout the year and has opened another location in Lisbon. And customers are curious. At least for one night, they want to have an experience out of the ordinary. They expect the worst and are not disappointed. This has been going on for 15 years already, although in recent years the hotel has slightly improved its service. Slightly only because it has a reputation to uphold, of course...

Big Apple, small car

It's the year 1959. 14 years after the end of the Second World War. In the United States, we see the big picture. Chrysler, Cadillac, Pontiac, and Buick cars are imposing, flashy, powerful, muscular, and large. Car advertising campaigns are colorful, high-sounding, filled with huge logos, and technical information. 1959 is the year when New York advertising agency Doyle Dane Bernbach's (DDB), founded by Bill Bernbach, receives a budget of $800,000 to sell the **Volkswagen Beetle** to the Americans. A big challenge that Julian Koenig, the DDB copywriter, summed up in one sentence: *"We're going to sell a Nazi car in the biggest Jewish city in the world."*

To carry out its mission, the advertising agency decided to go against the flow of what was done at the time. They highlighted the weaknesses of the product, but with humor! Yes, the Beetle is small. Yes, the Beetle is not very pretty. Yes, the Beetle is German. Yes, the Beetle was

Picture on top: Magazine advertisements for the Volkswagen Beetle in the late fifties.

designed to be "the car for the poor". All these characteristics - not really attractive - were condensed into a now legendary advertisement: a small black car lost on a white background with a short and simple slogan: *"Think small."* This offbeat visual catches the eye. It intrigues, it surprises. And it sparks the desire of the consumer. Other messages implicitly conveyed by the campaign are: *"Volkswagen does not lie about the product. You are confident. You know what you're buying. You are economical and clever."* Success came quickly. In the land of excess, the friendly Beetle became the Queen. Sales in the United States exceeded all expectations in the 60s. In 1972, it was to become the best-selling car in the world, a record until then held by the Ford Model T.

The uglier, the better

Large deformed carrots, odd-looking beans, twisted peppers, battered apples, three-headed lemons. Most of these out-of-the-ordinary-looking fruits and vegetables can only be found in "organic" stores. Supermarkets, on the other hand, allow little latitude for variations. Except at **Intermarché**. In 2014, the French chain of supermarket stores decided to sell these ugly, but other than that fresh and good tasting products. It launched an advertising campaign - which also relied on humor - to promote their minor flaws. And this commitment to curb food wastage continued, including the sale of ugly canned vegetables and ugly biscuits. These products are sold 30% cheaper than conventional products. In 2014, the "ugly fruits and vegetables" campaign managed to sell 1,600 tons of fruit and vegetables inside of 3 days.

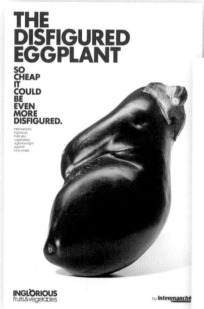

Today the initiative is regularly renewed and with a lot of success. Intermarché also sold 4 tons of ugly biscuits in November 2015 and 6.5 tons in June 2016. The supplier managed to rhyme ugly and funny, and ugly and delicious. It, therefore, saved excellent products from going to waste, while allowing customers to save some money.

LEARNINGS & IDEAS

This is your free space to reflect on what the previous story might have taught you and how you can use this knowledge in your own (work) environment. Let the questions here below stimulate you, take a pen and start writing!

- Do you know your weaknesses? And can you turn them into strenghts with humour and creativity?
- Can you use your underdog position as a USP? Can you convert your vulnerability into a quality? What tone of voice will you use? And which target group is ready to embrace it?

THE
RIVER

The River

A metaphorical view on an obstacle
and six ways to approach it

TECHNIQUE IN BRIEF ON PAGE 184

Imagine, you're running through the woods towards a well-defined goal. All of a sudden, a wide and wild river crosses your path. It comes as a surprise, and you're not prepared for it, but you're determined: you definitively want to reach your goal. What are you going to do?

The above is a familiar scenario for all of us who have ever worked on a specific project. Of course, the river symbolizes the unforeseen obstacle that crosses our path. It can be anything, but for sure it is a constraint that seems to obstruct our straight path towards our goal. And we have to find a solution. There's no giving up, no turning back.

This creativity technique, accompanied by a printed graph, is entirely focused on problem solving. Metaphorically speaking, there are six options: you can swim, bridge, block, bypass, sail or fish in the river. On the next page you will find an intentionally short and general explanation of what these verbs stand for.

Some of the options might initially sound a bit weird but try to take the metaphor as widely as possible. Also, the ideas coming from one option might also derive from another. Don't worry about that. In the end, it doesn't matter what 'impulse' made you come up with the idea as long as it's original and valuable.

1. SWIM the river

Are you strong and courageous enough to swim across the river, on your own or with others? Can you conquer or control the obstacle with power, energy, authority, drive and/or influence? Do you have everything you need for this or can you count on the help of others? Then put on your swimsuit, warm up, dive into the river and safely reach the other side.

2. BRIDGE the river

Do you have all the skills, materials, tools and insights to build a bridge across the river? Can you leave the obstacle untouched, but overpass it by constructing a smart connection that spans the gap between where you are now and where you want to be? Do you have everything you need for this or can you count on the help of others? Then start constructing a strong bridge that will bring you to the other side of the river!

3. BLOCK the river

Are you persuasive and persevering enough to block the river temporarily or for good? Can you prevent the obstacle to hinder your ambition by putting an end to it, deactivate or disarm it? Can this be done permanently or just for a short period of time? Do you have everything you need for this or can you count on the help of others? Then start building a dam right away, so that no more water runs through the river and you can easily wade through it!

4. BYPASS the river

Do you have the time, patience and lean mindset to walk around the river and bypass it? Is there any chance the obstacle will be less prominent under certain circumstances or at a specific point in time? Can you steer this in any way or do you just have to wait for the right moment? And how will you be able to take advantage of it to reach your goal? Then let go for a while and be patient but start planning your ultimate move strategically right away!

5. SAIL the river

Are you flexible and adventurous enough to sail the river and go with the flow? Can you initially accept the obstacle and go along with it to see where it will take you? Are you able to adapt your actions while never losing sight of your goal? Are you willing to take risks, be opportunistic, and change plans regularly? Then build a boat that you can easily navigate to ultimately reach your goal under the most volatile of conditions!

6. FISH the river

Do you have the smart and creative mindset to accept the river and go fishing in it? Have you ever considered that not the initial target you had in mind, but the obstacle itself might be your ultimate goal? Can you not only accept the obstacle but also embrace it as a true advantage, the USP you were looking for? And are you mad and creative enough to make it happen? Then take your fishing line, hang plenty of bait from it and get the biggest and tastiest of fish out of the water!

You can try this technique on your own, but as with any other technique in this book, it's much more fun and effective when you perform as a team (as described below). You can download The River graph at www.whentheboxisthelimit.com/river

SWIM
THE RIVER

Are you strong and courageous enough
to swim across the river, on your own or
with others?

 BRIDGE
THE RIVER

Do you have all the skills, materials,
tools and insights to build a bridge
across the river?

 BLOCK
THE RIVER

Are you persuasive and persevering
enough to block the river temporarily
or for good?

 BYPASS
THE RIVER

Do you have the time, patience and
lean mindset to walk around the river
and bypass it?

 SAIL
THE RIVER

Are you flexible and adventurous
enough to sail the river and go with the
flow?

 FISH
THE RIVER

Do you have the smart and creative
mindset to accept the river and go
fishing in it?

↓ ↓ ↓
select and develop the best ideas

The River.

WHENTHEBOXISTHELIMIT.COM

How it works:

It is recommended working with a group of at least six participants in a session, but it can just as easily be more.

STEP 1

- Print the graph on a large size sheet of paper, minimum A2, but bigger is better, certainly when working in groups.

- Put the sheet on the table or hang it on the wall. See what works best for you / your team.

- Provide post-its to everyone.

- Provide a regular die (with numbers from 1 to 6).

STEP 2

- Discuss the process and target you will work on, and make sure that everyone understands them clearly. Now discuss the obstacle that blocks you from reaching your goal. Bear in mind that this obstacle is your 'River'.

- Limit yourself to one obstacle at a time. If there are more, you can go through the process again at a later stage or use a second graph simultaneously, that may be handled by another team where relevant, appropriate or necessary.

STEP 3

- Make teams of two or more people (depending on the total number of participants in the session), with a maximum of four teams per session.

- Each team now rolls the die. The number they throw corresponds with the option they will work on that is mentioned in the printed graph. For instance, if a team throws a 3, they will start working on the option 'BLOCK the river'.

STEP 4

- Try to separate the teams a bit so they won't disturb each other. You might foresee small tables and chairs along the outside wall of the room.

- *Start the clock: during the next 6 minutes each team will generate ideas according to the received option (the number they rolled with the die). They will write their ideas down on post-its they do not share with the group yet.*

- *When the clock stops, each team sticks and presents its ideas to the right of the respective option on the sheet.*

STEP 5

- *The group can decide to keep the same teams or to change them. Anyhow, we repeat STEP 3 and*

STEP 4. If a team or team member gets an option assigned they already worked on the team rolls the die again.

- *According to your number of participants, you can repeat these steps several times. It is important that ALL of the options have been addressed by at least two teams.*

STEP 6

- *When you decide to stop the session, select the best ideas on the sheet and start developing them into concepts.*

"No one has ever succeeded in crossing a river by waiting until it has passed by or dried out."

(African proverb)

WHEN THE STAKES ARE HIGH

WAR! huh, yeah.
What is it good for?
Absolutely something...

In the early seventies, Edwin Starr sang with full conviction that war was good for nothing. *'Absolutely nothing!'* his fellow hippies yelled along with him. Of course, because... don't we all dream of a world without war? It is therefore with a lot of pain in my heart – as a committed pacifist – that I can't agree with him wholeheartedly. As much as war brings out the worst in human beings, it is at the same time a setting where creativity often thrives. And that is not surprising. Extreme situations – with severe constraints as a consequence - force us to leave the beaten path and look for entirely new solutions.

Sometimes it is all about a simple 'rethinking' of the problem, which is meant to circumvent imposed restrictions and protocols; for instance, with ration coupons for food or curfews after a particular hour. In other cases, it is about sheer individual survival. Think about the ingenuity of people hiding from or escaping the enemy, or looking for food and shelter. All are situations where we employ our most creative instincts. All of the scenarios above seldomly generate ideas that would work in times of peace because it is usually not about products or services, but rather situational, individual, and temporary solutions.

It is different when problems are dealt with in an organized manner and on a larger scale. In times of war, the military machine is in full swing, so it is no miracle that most wartime inventions spring from this well. The stakes are high and time is limited, so the pressure to come up with creative solutions is huge. Whether it is about outwitting the enemy, sending supplies to the troops, or tending to the wounded, wartime inventions are of all times. This is true of all times, from the Greek scientist Archimedes in the second century BCE, who thought of the catapult to fight the enemy from afar, to the invention of today's high-tech drones that can be programmed to kill people based on facial recognition.

Luckily, not all inventions are lethal. On the contrary, some have improved our daily comfort greatly, while others outright changed the face of this earth. In short, we often don't fully realize how many everyday products and services that we benefit from today were born out of the constricting straightjacket of war and conflict.

The Internet

At the time of the launch of the Sputnik I by the former Soviet Union, it became clear to the United States that they were not as almighty and invulnerable as they thought they were in the period after the Second World War. As an immediate response to the launch, the Advanced Research Projects Agency (ARPA) was founded within the American Ministry of Defense. The ARPA had to take care of the development of technology that would enable the American defense forces not to be blindsided and sandbagged by a technologically advanced enemy. That's why the ARPA think tank developed an efficient way to connect computer systems at different locations to have them communicate

The front panel of first Interface Message Processor used to interconnect participant networks to the ARPANET from the late 1960s to 1989

"We don't realize how many everyday products and services were born out of the constricting straightjacket of war and conflict."

with each other. They developed a system - which they called ARPANET - that separated information into small packages that were sent via the best and safest routes to their destinations individually. At the destinations, those packages were re-assembled into the original message.

Although the original idea was already put to paper in 1962, the first real connection was not made until seven years later. And it was only in the early 1980s, that the Internet was pulled from the military corner, only to really reach larger audiences in the early 1990s.

Sanitary Pads

Cellucotton, a fiber that is five times as absorbent as cotton, was already invented before the First World Word by Kimberly-Clark, then a small American company. When the United States sent soldiers to the front lines in Europe in 1917, the absorbing cotton wool by Kimberly-Clark was manufactured quickly to use as a surgical material to staunch the blood. The end of the war in 1918 caused a temporary adjournment of the cotton wool activities of Kimberly-Clark because its most important clients – the army and the Red Cross – had no need for the product anymore. So they went looking for a new market.

Early KOTEX ads that appeared in the period between the two world wars

The nurses on the battlefields had discovered the advantages of the material for their personal hygiene. It was this unofficial use that paved the way to success for the company. After two years of intensive development, the company brought the first sanitary pads to market, made of Cellucotton and fine gauze. The new product was named Kotex, which was short for 'cotton-textile'. And actually, it is crazy to think that today – nearly 100 years later – the product has never been disruptively innovated. An untapped market?

Vegetarian Sausage

"Sauerkraut, Wurst und Bratkartoffeln." Each country has its culinary clichés, and Germany is – at least when it comes to perception – not exactly in the top three countries with a fine, creative, and healthy gastronomy. The culinary specialty of Berlin is, therefore, the Curry Wurst itself. In fact, they have even established a museum for it. In brief, Germans love Wurst.

The vegetarian sausage was invented by former German Chancellor Conrad Adenauer.

When Conrad Adenauer – the first Federal Chancellor of the Second World War – still was mayor of Cologne in 1917, he had to find a solution for the food shortages resulting from the English blockade at the end of the First World War. With his inventive mind, he looked for alternatives to the already very popular bratwurst, because meat was in short supply. He made a mix of rice flour, barley, and Rumanian corn flour. It all seemed to work until Rumania declared war, and the supply of corn flour dried up. Out of necessity, he went looking for a new ingredient as a meat-replacement, and he ended up with soy. In the end, it appeared to be an even better choice than the Rumanian corn flour. The product was called 'Friedenswurst' or peace sausage.

Adenauer applied for a patent on it with the imperial patent bureau in Germany, but he was denied because the content of his sausage was in conflict with the German laws on the right content for a sausage (a sausage had to contain at least some meat). Oddly enough, he had better luck in Great-Britain, then the German enemy. King George V granted the soy-sausage a patent on 26 June 1918.

Duct Tape

During the Second World War, the American troops had a very impractical way of reloading their weapons. The shells for grenade launchers were packed in a carton box, which was sealed with wax, and fully taped to protect them against moisture. In the heat of the battle, it was not easy for a soldier to reload his weapon, and the enemy could benefit from that.

Vesta Stoudt was the mother of two American soldiers at the frontline and worked in a factory that inspected and packed those shells. Concerned for the wellbeing of her two sons, she suggested to her boss that they produce tape made of strong, water resistant fabric. When her boss blew her off, she wrote a letter (with a hand-drawn sketch of the product) to President Franklin Roosevelt, requesting urgent support for her idea. Roosevelt handed Stoudt's suggestion to his military staff, and not long after that, she got a letter in return with the message that her proposal was approved.

In the end, it was Johnson & Johnson who were awarded the development and production of the product. There are different stories about the name's origin. Some sources claim that the product was originally named 'duck-tape' by the soldiers who used it, because water had no hold on it, and the drops washed off just as it did off the feathers of a duck. Shortly after the war, the company launched a silver version of it named 'duct tape' after engineers discovered the product could also be used to seal heating ducts.

Duct tape: invented by a worried mother, approved by the American President.

LEARNINGS & IDEAS

This is your free space to reflect on what the previous story might have taught you and how you can use this knowledge in your own (work) environment. Let the questions here below stimulate you, take a pen and start writing!

- Under extreme pressure from the competitor, which daily processes and routines do you have to 'rethink' ?
- What can you learn from your 'warriors' in the field? Which kind of constraints do they encounter? What kind of 'weapons' can you develop for them to fight with? And can you re-use these weapons for other purposes?

OPEN THAT BOX!

Why more and more organizations choose
Open Innovation

These days, you don't have to convince too many entrepreneurs that creativity and innovation are essential to maintain an advantage over your competition and in the market. In many cases, it's not even about keeping an advantage, but merely trying to keep up with the rhythm and not fall behind hopelessly. "Innovate or die" is a slogan that has been flying around for the last few years. The plethora of initiatives taken on by organizations and businesses to effectively innovate prove that this slogan has not landed on deaf ears. However, when an innovation strategy is being launched, it is mainly aimed at the innovation capacity available in-house. In other words, the whole process takes place internally. This is probably to avoid leaks that the competition could use to its advantage.

Innovation most often is about a classic closed model. This model takes into account the limitations that are inherent to the organization. That goes from research to implementation, from creative potential to the capacity to develop innovative ideas and to test, adjust, and implement them. To successfully complete all of these steps, an organization needs a lot of resources. But not everyone – and certainly not all smaller organizations or companies – has this arsenal of weapons. Metaphorically speaking: you need a helluva big toolbox to build a house all by yourself.

If the box is too small, open it!

To face the internal limitations and obstacles head on, more and more entrepreneurs find the way to **open innovation**. In his book *'Open Innovation: The New Imperative for Creating and Profiting from Technology'*, Dr. Henry Chesbrough introduces a model that allows use of internal as well as external means to shape innovation. When you extrapolate the metaphor above, you could say: if you don't have all the tools in your own toolbox, don't be too proud to borrow what you need from the neighbours. The main idea behind open innovation is that in our present world, where creativity, knowledge, and skills are so widespread, we can't afford to depend only on our own internal capabilities.

You find Chesbrough's model here below:

CLOSED INNOVATION PRINCIPLES	OPEN INNOVATION PRINCIPLES
The smart people in the field work for us.	Not all the smart people work for us, so one must find and tap into the knowledge and expertise of bright individuals outside our company.
To profit from R&D, we must discover it, develop it, and ship it ourselves.	External R&D can create significant value: internal R&D is needed to claim some portion of that value.
If we discover it ourselves, we will get it to the market first.	We don't have to originate the research to profit from it.
The company that gets an innovation to the market first will win.	Building a better business model is better than getting to the market first.
If we create the most and the best ideas in the industry, we will win.	If we make the best use of internal and external ideas, we will win.
We should control our intellectual property (IP) so that our competitors don't profit from our ideas.	We should profit from others' use of our IP, and we should buy others' IP whenever it advances our business model.

Three examples

In our present interconnected world, open innovation offers a lot of chances to lower the cost of research, spread risk, and market innovation faster. A recent article about open innovation that was published by the World Economic Forum features some concrete examples.

1. With the project "Open Access Malaria Box", Medicine Malaria Venture offers access to 400 configurations with anti-malaria properties. In exchange for the use of this box, the organization asks that the results based on this information be shared publicly to make new configurations for drugs accessible for everybody. This has contributed to the development of new medication against malaria and sleeping sickness.

2. Another example stems from the IT branch. Here open innovation has led to companies licensing each other's software to build new products. This saves licensing organizations and their end users considerable cost. Two very successful examples of this model are Android and Apple platforms. Those have led to a large number of innovative services that are based on it.

3. But authorities embrace the open innovation model too. In this article, an example is featured from the United Kingdom where in 2012 the non-profit Open Data Institute funds companies with £10 million government money to encourage them to innovate by way of publicly shared data. By researching the prescription practice of the National Health Service, they could prove that doctors prescribed £27m per month worth of expensive pharmaceutical brand products instead of cheaper and equally effective generic medication. Dealing with this problem would save the country £200 million annually.

TESLA OPENED THE BOX

In mid 2014, Elon Musk, CEO of electrical car manufacturer Tesla, announced that the company was going to release all its patents open and free of charge on the market. On the Tesla website, you can find the following statement: *"Tesla Motors was created to accelerate the advent of sustainable transport. If we clear a path to the creation of compelling electric vehicles, but then lay intellectual property landmines behind us to inhibit others, we are acting in a manner contrary to that goal. Tesla will not initiate patent lawsuits against anyone who, in good faith, wants to use our technology."*

A true revolution in the automotive industry where competition is killing and where – like in many other technology driven sectors – protectionism has been perfected to an art form. Open innovation may have been birthed by the presence of (internal) limitation the model now grows into the single most important win-win model of the future where one plus one makes three.

To quote Musk one more time: *"Technology leadership is not defined by patents, which history has repeatedly shown to be small protection indeed against a determined competitor, but rather by the ability of a company to attract and motivate the world's most talented engineers. We believe that applying the open source philosophy to our patents will strengthen rather than diminish Tesla's position in this regard."*

"It is the long history of human kind that those who learned to collaborate and improvise most effectively have prevailed."

Charles Darwin

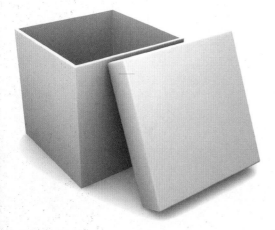

The
Constraint
Suite.

An overview of the
five creativity techniques
that turn constraints into
creative ideas

The Frugalizor.

PAGE 42

WHAT IS IT?

Based on the idea of **frugal innovation** (= making products and services available and affordable to the masses with limited resources), you will enhance your product or service via twelve frugal mechanisms.

WHEN TO USE?

The Frugalizor is developed for a broad kind of applications. If you want to enhance a product, a service, a process, a structure, an idea, a design, a vision or any other form of innovation issue you are working on, then give it a go. The focus is on frugal, which means that you might consider making your 'subject' more available and afordable to a large target group with limited resources.

WHERE DO I FIND MORE INFO?

You can find a full description of the technique on pages 42 to 49.

WHAT DO I NEED?

- 4 to 12 participants recommended

- 45 to 90 minutes of time

- Post-its and pens

- The Frugalizor poster + The Frugalizor tent cards, both downloadable on www.whentheboxisthelimit.com/frugalizor

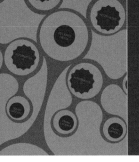

Tree of Trade.

PAGE 62

WHAT IS IT?

Tree of Trade is a technique that is built on **thinking in alternatives**. Your goal is to replace essential elements of your subject by creative alternatives that cater the same needs.

WHEN TO USE?

The technique is an ideal mindstretcher to enhance products, services, processes or any other form of innovation issue you are working on. Participants who have an open mind will generate quite surprising and creative ideas with this technique.

WHERE DO I FIND MORE INFO?

You can find a full description of the technique on pages 62 to 66.

WHAT DO I NEED?

- 4 to 10 participants recommended
- 45 to 90 minutes of time
- Post-its and pens
- Tree of Trade poster, downloadable on
  www.whentheboxisthelimit.com/treeoftrade

The Propeller.

PAGE 106

WHAT IS IT?

This technique allows you to analyse the constraint(s) you're facing, by digging deeper into it. On the other side, The Propeller will lift you up and give you a clear overview of the challenge you're facing.

WHEN TO USE?

Use The Propeller when you are stuck in a problem or challenge because of a certain obstacle. By asking why it restricts you to reach your goal (in several layers), you will discover the essence of the obstacle and find an alternative solution for it. The technique also stimulates you to finetune your ideas and translate them into real and applicable solutions.

WHERE DO I FIND MORE INFO?

You can find a full description of the technique on pages 106 to 111.

WHAT DO I NEED?

- 4 to 12 participants recommended
- 60 to 120 minutes of time
- Small post-its and pens
- The Propeller poster, downloadable on www.whentheboxisthelimit.com/propeller

The Casual Constraint Contest

PAGE 124

WHAT IS IT?

A highly activating team game, combining **teamwork**, **competition** and **restrictions**, the magic mix for generating great ideas quickly.

WHEN TO USE?

The Casual Constraint Contest allows you to generate disruptive and distinctive ideas to start innovating your product, your service, your organisation. At the same time, the competition element enhances the team spirit of the participants.

WHERE DO I FIND MORE INFO?

You can find a full description of the technique on pages 124 to 129.

WHAT DO I NEED?

- 6 to 12 participants recommended (preferably a multiple of 3)

- 60 to 90 minutes of time

- Post-its and pens

- The 'What if' constraint cards + a six-color dice + a number of red, yellow and blue pawns, all downloadable or purchaseable on www.whentheboxisthelimit.com/casualconstraintcontest

The River.

PAGE 156

WHAT IS IT?

By using a river that crosses your path as a metaphor, you are obliged to find a solution to reach your goal on the other side of the river. There are six options that will guide you.

WHEN TO USE?

This creativity technique is entirely focused on problem solving. Metaphorically speaking, you get six options: you can swim, bridge, block, bypass, sail or fish the river. Use it when you're stuck in a certain process. The river symbolises the obstacle that blocks you and with at least one of the options, you will find your way to overcome the obstacle.

WHERE DO I FIND MORE INFO?

You can find a full description of the technique on pages 156 to 162.

WHAT DO I NEED?

- 6 to 18 participants recommended
- 60 to 120 minutes of time
- Post-its and pens
- The River poster, downloadable on www.whentheboxisthelimit.com/river

Discover **more**

Download the **tools** that
come with the **thechniques**

WWW.**WHENTHEBOXISTHELIMIT**.COM

Become a certified **trainer**

Be part of the growing **community**
and share your **insights**

REFERENCE list of books and articles

- The Journal of Consumer Research – Vol 42, Issue5, February 2016 - Creating When You Have Less: The Impact of Resource Scarcity on Product Use Creativity

- Dezeen – Architecture and Design Magazine – Rima Sabina Aouf – August 2016

- Website http://www.ikeahackers.net

- Notesofnomads.com - New life to an old phone booth: London's smallest library - April 2014

- BBC News - Phone boxes turn green to charge mobiles – October 2014

- Business Insider - An entrepreneur is selling salad out of an old London phone booth – May 2016

- Frugal Innovation - How to do better with less - by Navi Radjou and Jaideep Prabhu - February 2015

- Jugaadking.blogspot.com - The Six Principles of Jugaad – August 2012

- Open Culture - The (Urban) Legend of Ernest Hemingway's Six-Word Story - by Josh Jones - March 2015

- Journal of Innovation and Entrepreneurship - Research and development from the bottom up - introduction of terminologies for new product development in emerging markets - Alexander Brem and Pierre Wolfram – September 2013.

- Open Innovation: The New Imperative for Creating and Profiting from Technology - Henry William Chesbrough - 2003

- Website http://http://www.sundropfarms.com

- Harvard Business Review – Breakthrough thinking from inside the box – by Kevin Coyne, Patricia Gorman Clifford and Renée Dye – December 2007

- Hubspot - The Surprising Relationship Between Stress and Creativity - by Braden Becker – February 2018

- The Mission - Parkinson's Law: Why Constraints Are The Best Thing You Can Work With – by Lewis Chew – May 2017

- Website http://www.theshoethatgrows.org

- Inside the box: A proven system of creativity for breakthrough results – by Drew Boyd and Jacob Goldenbergh

- A Beautiful Constraint: How To Transform Your Limitations Into Advantages, and Why It's Everyone's Business – by Adam Morgan and Marc Barden

- Widewalls Editorial - Cardboard Art and Its Many Forms – by Eli Anapur and Elena Martinique – Sepetember 2016

- Rice Galery - Ana Serrano: Salon of Beauty – by Melody Soto – May 2014

- Website http://www.wheelchairsofhope.org

- Website http://www.openwheelchair.org

- Journal of Personality and Social Psychology - Stepping back to see the big picture: when obstacles elicit global processing – by Marguc J, Förster J, Van Kleef GA – November 2011

- Website http:// www.tipoonthetravelmachine.com

- Unmissablejapan.com - Manga Kissa

- Website https://aerofarms.com

- Le Parisien - Romainville : bientôt la première «tour maraîchère» de France - by Elsa Marnette - June 2018

- The Washington Post - 'Houston, we have a problem': The amazing history of the iconic Apollo 13 misquote - by Michael S. Rosenwald - April 2017

- Website http://www.dyson.com
- The Rebel Surgeon - a movie by Erik Gandini - 2018
- Website http://www.cirquedusoleil.com
- Chicago Children's Museum - Mr Imagine's Toy Store - December 2012
- The Wall Street Journal - Tour Embraces a Town's Ugly Truth: It's a Dump - by Frances Robinson - December 2010
- Website https://hansbrinker.com
- Design Shack - The Greatest Print Campaigns of All Time: Volkswagen Think Small - by Joshua Johnson - October 2017
- Paris Match - Quand les fruits et légumes moches font recette dans l'assiette - by Kathleen Wuyard - November 2017
- BBC News - 10 inventions that owe their success to World War One - by Stephen Evans - April 2014
- Harvard Business Review - Open Innovation Generates Great Ideas, So Why Aren't Companies Adopting Them? - by Dirk Deichmann, Ieva Rozentale and Robert Barnhoorn - December 2017
- Forbes - Everything You Need to Know About Open Innovation - by Henry Chesbrough - March 2011
- World Economic Forum - The benefits of open innovation - by Elie Chachoua - February 2015
- Fast Company - The Science Of Why Scarcity Makes Us More Creative - by Charlie Sorrel - January 2015
- CNN - Jazz improv and your brain: The key to creativity? - By Sandee LaMotte - April 2018
- Psychology Today - Does Creativity Require Constraints? - by Barry Kaufman - August 2011
- CNN - Enter India's amazing world of frugal innovation - by Arion McNicoll - September 2014
- Website http://www.mitticool.com
- Nautilus - The 6 Most Surprising, Important Inventions From World War I - by Simone Sculy - October 2014
- Website http://www.playpumps.co.za
- Centre for frugal innovation in Africa - Frugal Innovation in Practice - Frugal Weather Stations - February 2018
- The Economist - Why does Kenya lead the world in mobile money? - March 2015
- Huffpost - Billboard In Lima, Peru Creates Drinking Water Out Of Thin Air - by Jessica Prois - March 2013
- New Atlas - Be-Bound app provides mobile internet access without 3G or Wi-Fi - by Stu Robarts - November 2013
- Website http://www.dacia.com
- Domino - 20 Epic Ikea Hacks You Can Easily Tackle - by Anna Kocharian - May 2018
- The Telegraph - Bed in a box: the world's coolest capsule hotels - by Charlotte Johnstone - April 2018
- Website http://www.polarcircles.com
- Business Insider - Here's how Uber got its start and grew to become the most valuable startup in the world - by Nathan McAlone - September 2015
- Deutsche Welle - New mobility for people living with disability in DRC - by Simone Schlindwein - August 2016
- The Dieline - Designer Lisanne Koning Thinks Inside the Box for Refugee Children - by Bill McCool - November 2017
- Inhabitat - Chris Gilmour Transforms Recycled Cardboard into Life-Size Sculptures of Dentist Chairs and Pianos - by Lori Zimmer - April 2012

IMAGE COURTESY

p17   Image Courtesy Depositphoto

p21   Image Courtesy Depositphoto

p23   Image Courtesy Depositphoto

p24   Image Courtesy Depositphoto

p26   Image Courtesy Pixabay

p29   Image Courtesy Culture Images/Hollandse Hoogte

p30   Image Courtesy Meter Group, Inc

p32   Image Courtesy MittaCool

p33   Image Courtesy UTEC

p34   Image Courtesy M-KOPA

p34   Image Courtesy TAHMO

p35   Image Courtesy Depositphoto and Be-Bound

p35   Image Courtesy Renault

p37   Image Courtesy Depositphoto

p38/39 Image Courtesy Depositphoto

p40/41 Image Courtesy Kenton Lee

p42   Image Courtesy Depositphoto

p45   Image Courtesy Depositphoto

p50   Image Courtesy Depositphoto

p52   Image Courtesy Depositphoto

p54   Image Courtesy Depositphoto

p55   Image Courtesy Depositphoto

p56   Image Courtesy Depositphoto

p58   Image Courtesy IKEA and Pinterest

p59   Image Courtesy IKEA, Reinventing IKEA and FabShop

p60   Image Courtesy Pinterest

p61   Image Courtesy IKEA and Ikeahackers.net

p66   Image Courtesy Depositphoto

p67   Image Courtesy G.K. Chesterton

p68   Image Courtesy Depositphoto

p69   Image Courtesy Depositphoto

p70   Image Courtesy Depositphoto

p71   Image Courtesy Depositphoto

p73   Image Courtesy Depositphoto

p74   Image Courtesy Depositphoto

p75   Image Courtesy Depositphoto

p76   Image Courtesy Cyril Parkinson

p78   Image Courtesy Yousuf Karsh

p81   Image Courtesy Depositphoto

p82   Image Courtesy Pinterest

p83   Image Courtesy Typoon

p84   Image Courtesy Typoon

p85   Image Courtesy First Cabin

p85   Image Courtesy Narita Airport Capsule Hotel

p86   Image Courtesy Book and Bed Tokio

p87   Image Courtesy AeroFarms

p88   Image Courtesy ILIMELGO

p89   Image Courtesy Frank Lloyd Wright

p90   Image Courtesy Depositphoto

p91   Image Courtesy Depositphoto

p92   Image Courtesy Lovefoon

p93   Image Courtesy Solarbox

p94   Image Courtesy Spier's Salads

p95   Image Courtesy Pinterest

p96   Image Courtesy Polar Circles

p99   Image Courtesy Polar Circles

p100   Image Courtesy Depositphoto

p100   Image Courtesy Sioen and Polar Circles

p102   Image Courtesy NASA

p104   Image Courtesy NASA

p105   Image Courtesy Depositphoto

p106   Image Courtesy Depositphoto

p108   Image Courtesy Depositphoto

p109   Image Courtesy Depositphoto

p111   Image Courtesy Depositphoto

p112   Image Courtesy Depositphoto

p114   Image Courtesy Reuters

115   Image Courtesy Dyson

p116   Image Courtesy Cirque du Soleil

p116   Image Courtesy Jens Alaene/DPA/Zuma Press

p117   Image Courtesy la.curbed.com

p119   Image Courtesy Depositphoto

p120   Image Courtesy Depositphoto

p122   Image Courtesy Depositphoto

p124   Image Courtesy Depositphoto

p126   Image Courtesy Depositphoto

p129   Image Courtesy Depositphoto

p130   Image Courtesy Depositphoto

p132   Image Courtesy SunDrops

p133   Image Courtesy SunDrops

p134   Image Courtesy Fasad Cine ab

p135   Image Courtesy Fasad Cine ab

p136   Image Courtesy Fasad Cine ab

p137   Image Courtesy Depositphoto

p138   Image Courtesy OpenWheelchair.org

p139   Image Courtesy OpenWheelchair.org

p140   Image Courtesy WheelchairsOfHope.org

p141   Image Courtesy Foundation-Mboyo

p142   Image Courtesy Depositphoto

p144   Image Courtesy Lisanne Koning

p145   Image Courtesy Chicago Children's Museum

p146   Image Courtesy Ana Serano

p147   Image Courtesy Chris Gilmour

p148   Image Courtesy Depositphoto

p150   Image Courtesy Wonderfriends

p151   Image Courtesy Hans Brinker Hotel

p152   Image Courtesy Depositphoto

p153   Image Courtesy Volkswagen

p154   Image Courtesy Intermarché

p155   Image Courtesy Depositphoto

p156   Image Courtesy Depositphoto

p160   Image Courtesy Depositphoto

p162   Image Courtesy Depositphoto

p164   Image Courtesy Depositphoto

p166   Image Courtesy Arpanet

p168   Image Courtesy Kotex

p169   Image Courtesy Depositphoto

p170   Image Courtesy Depositphoto

p171   Image Courtesy Depositphoto

p172   Image Courtesy Depositphoto

p175   Image Courtesy Pinterest

p176   Image Courtesy Tesla

p177   Image Courtesy Charles Darwin

p178   Image Courtesy Depositphoto

p179   Image Courtesy Depositphoto

Thanks a million!

It was a great journey. And although writing is usually a solitary trip, I am a lucky man to have met many good-hearted and capable people on my path. I can not thank you enough for everything you have done:

My colleagues and students at the Erasmus University College Brussels, always willing to lend an ear and giving their thoughts and encouragements on my writing project.

Thomas Calis, Vanessa Toelen, Philippe Vandenameele, Ingrid Schroyens, Kris Debisschop en Sophie Van Steene for giving valuable feedback on the creativity techniques I designed.

Ramon Vullings and Cyriel Kortleven for their priceless advice on the do's and dont's of writing a book on creativity and everything that comes with it.

Marc Heleven for the thorough research and the inspiring conversations that have filled this book with tons of interesting cases.

Bionda Dias and Sara van de Ven for their support and dedication as publishers of the book.

Bernandak and Tania Cohen for their accurate text editing and translation.

My two children Flo and Viktor for their never-ending support, their valuable ideas and their unconditional love.

My lovely wife Estelle for about everything I did and did not mention yet: without your love and continuous support, I could never have done it.